Evelyn's story has practical ap
sustainable relationship with Jes
Her journal is a careful reflection .... by the Holy
Spirit.
Tony Wood, CEO, Carmen Ministries

I once heard it said that when love decides the moment, God
shows up. Evelyn has done an outstanding job highlighting the
driving theme of the Bible in its entirety and God's heart from
the very beginning - It all can be summed up in one word: Love.
She beautifully weaves in the concepts of intimacy, worship, and
understanding the tenderness of the heart of God. Are you looking
to more fully understand the loving heart of God and to be more
fully understood by God in His fullest - Father, Son, and Holy Spirit?
Then I wholeheartedly recommend this wonderful book.
Rev. Daniel P. Quagliata, Lead Pastor
The Bridge Church
Malverne, NY

"Evelyn Lang has found a way to express the Father's love in her
new book "A Lifetime Of Love" which has an easy to digest format.
Its simplicity is profound. Its reading is smooth and carefully crafted.
It is written in such a way that the simple and astute person will both
glean something of great value from it. It is a tremendous blessing
to the Kingdom of God. Anyone who is looking to learn more about
God's love through relationships needs to read this book. "
Pastor Anthony Gambino
Lead Pastor, Crossroads Church
Hamburg, NJ
www.crossroadshamburg.com

One's spiritual development is often woefully neglected even
though it has been shown to be the basis of genuine serenity,
successful relationships and the courage to change. The chapters
of this book are generously written from prayerful moments of
reflection between Evelyn and God. As a result you will find
countless gems of wisdom in settings of clarity, introspection,
practicality and humor. I highly recommend this book for anyone

seeking the only One who knows and loves you best through any and all circumstances.

Joanne J. Smith, MSW, LCSW, BCD, psychotherapist, Ringwood, New Jersey

What a beautiful, easy reading, and detailed description of love in its many dimensions.

This book helps us learn about our love relationship with God and as a by-product what true love is in our earth-bound relationships, especially in our marriages. It beautifully describes our Heavenly Father's love as a parent for His children and the love of Christ as a bridegroom for His bride. It discusses many issues in marriage such as the "blame game" and how to change feuding over finances to fairness.

The Lord has gifted Mrs. Lang with the ability to use common well known items to cleverly help us understand complex issues - like using a balloon to show us how to avoid dominant control in marriage, using hot chocolate to discuss one aspect of the Holy Spirit's work, and using an egg (with its white and yolk) to show different opinions by spouses as a good thing. And much more.

Jim Biscardi Jr., President Emeritus of New Jersey Christian Ministries

A Lifetime of Love will bless you as Evelyn explains about the deep love that the Lord has for us and the power of that love. What wonderful insight she gives on the beautiful relationship that the Father, Son and Holy Spirit long to have with us.

Andi Whitefield, Author - Learning To Fly and Recipes For the Heart

A Lifetime of
Love

The Love Relationship

Evelyn Lang

Dove
Publishers

Bladensburg, MD

A Lifetime of Love

Published by
Inscript Books
a division of Dove Christian Publishers
P.O. Box 611
Bladensburg, MD 20710-0611
www.dovechristianpublishers.com

Cover Design by Nadia Chatsworth

ISBN: 978-1-7348625-3-9

Library of Congress Control Number: 2020941123

Scriptures quotations, unless otherwise marked, are from the King James Version of the Bible, which is in the public domain.

Published in the United States of America

25 24 23 22 21 20   1 2 3 4 5

Dedication

To God, for His everlasting love

To My husband Bill, for a lifetime of love, I will love you always

Contents

Foreword

I have long believed in the biblical principle of love. Evelyn Lang has God's anointing and the leading of the Holy Spirit to tell this compelling story.

We met a few years ago on my television program called *It's Time for Herman and Sharron*. Evelyn and Bill just fit together. They were comfortable with each other and they had The Love Relationship. Since the interview, Bill has graduated. He is now experiencing complete love.

This book instructs the body of Christ, biblically and practically, how to have "a lifetime of love." Evelyn reminds us how much "the Lord loves to be with us." As you read the words, you will quickly realize this person has experienced "dream talk with the Lord." Evelyn loves the Lord in an unusual and personal way.

So let's take this read together, and enjoy *A Lifetime of Love*.

Herman Bailey
Executive Producer and Host
It's Time for Herman and Sharron

Acknowledgments

I would like to thank the editors at Inscript Books for their knowledge and help in publishing this book. I would especially like to thank Raenita, who answered dozens of questions with patience and understanding and for her kindness and efficiency in making this an easy and enjoyable experience. Many thanks to the copyeditors, designers, and marketing experts, who have worked so hard to bring this book to completion.

A big thank you to Pastor Anthony and Jennifer Gambino for encouraging me and giving me the confidence to move forward with this project. It is a priceless gift that is greatly appreciated.

To all my friends who have prayed faithfully for me throughout this whole process: you have lifted up my arms when I needed it most. Thank you for your friendship and care.

Thank you, Victor, who put in a great amount of work and time on my website when time was at a premium in your business.

To Pat and Brian, who gave up their time and rearranged their schedules to help me with my computer so that it would be ready for publishing this book. Thank you for blessing me.

Thank you, Lynn, for offering help with marketing. Your help is very appreciated.

To Nadia, the cover designer, with my thanks.

Introduction

When God told me that I would be writing a book on love, I wondered how this book would be any different from what is already out there. And what more could anyone need to know about love than they already know? Love is love, isn't it? I was surprised at what God had to tell me — how involved and complex love really is.

One would think that this book would be all gushy, but instead it is a "reality" book. Like so many of the new TV shows, this book gets down to the real and true and not just the "feel good fluff." It deals with real issues for real people and for real-life experiences. It is about the love relationship and the three facets of the Lord's love for us. It is about the Father's love for us as His child, Jesus' love for us as His bride, and the Holy Spirit's love for us as our comforter and friend. It deals with our spiritual love for God the Father, Son, and Holy Spirit as well as our earthly love for our spouses, families, friends, and it also addresses the hurts we may have from dealing with real, ordinary, everyday, imperfect people. (It has some gush, too.)

Sometimes we are at the Lord's feet, where He instructs us with His wisdom — where He teaches with love. Sometimes, we are in His lap when He comforts and holds us as a child. And sometimes we walk right beside Him, as He communicates to us as His friend, and as we carry out His plans.

Opening my eyes to it all has not always been easy, as God very often teaches me by experience. However, one thing has always been constant: God's great love for His people.

There are many books on love, but this one will get to the *heart* of it!

Chapter 1

Won't You Be My Valentine?

*L*ove — people tend to use the word so lightly — they love this dress, they love this food, they love this house, car, etc. So they don't always realize that when God says He loves them, His love is very deep. In fact, we can never really fully understand the extent of His love. When we get to heaven we'll know more, however, no human on earth can love as the Lord does. Love is everything. It is the answer to many problems. If everyone had love, there would be no crime, no hurting others. Love is the key.

Young people think that love is physical attraction. That's only the very start. Many give up on love when that physical attraction gets old, and the excitement and newness wear off. They carry this over to the Lord when the excitement and newness they feel for Him wears off. But love isn't just a feeling of lust or excitement when something is new. Love is a bond between two people that does not say what can you do for me, or how can you make me feel good — and then leaves if it does not get its way; rather, it says what can I do for you? It is giving, not taking. True love grows, but it does not grow *old*. It is a commitment that remains true, even when times get hard. If swans can mate for life, why can't people who are made in God's image? And why does their love for God grow cold?

I felt God's heart as He spoke to me about this very thing. God is the same. He does not change. But people can change in their emotions and feelings — even for Him. They grow tired of Him. They get angry with Him. How His heart aches when they turn away from Him in the night and look the other way during the day. What happened to their first love? Who turned their heads? But the Lord says that He has not looked the other way or turned from you. Where did you go? He waits with open arms. He says, "Come, let Me love you. Let Me draw you unto Myself. I desire you."

I think that love is all-encompassing to the Lord.

L = *life and more abundantly*
O = *no beginning, no end*
V = *victory*
E = *everlasting to everlasting-eternal*

We all get excited about God's love for us in the beginning when we are new in Christ. It is the beginning of the love relationship. But then sometimes as we go along in our walk, we get lukewarm. God's love is still there, but we don't sense it as much. We get used to it and desensitized to Him. When we get so familiar with someone, we can take them for granted. The same is true for spouses. We can start to take them for granted, but then something happens and we realize how much they mean to us. It's human nature. Always appreciate, always desire — or else we become blind to their love, blind to how they bless us. Sometimes we get so used to having the blessing and gift of them that it doesn't seem special anymore. But then if something happens to threaten the relationship, our eyes are opened. There is a saying that you never know what you had until you've lost it. I wonder if that's why God may step back sometimes, just to let us see how much we need Him, and by doing so, draws us closer to Him and rekindles our desire for Him. He steps back a bit because we can get so busy with everyday life that we lose sight of Him. He may step back at that time so that we realize that there's too much clutter and busyness. When we miss Him, we desire to reconnect with Him. He may do this as a safeguard so that we don't get too far away from Him. He wants us to seek Him. He wants to know how much we desire Him, but He also wants **us** to realize how much we desire Him, too.

At one season in my life, I was feeling like He was far from me, and I told Him that if I have to wrestle like Jacob, I will not let Him go. He told me that now I was getting it! Sometimes He steps back so that He knows *how much* we really want Him — enough to even fight for Him? The best things in life are worth fighting for; it shows how valuable they are. And if we, as dust, need to know that someone values us enough to fight for us, shouldn't we think that God may test us every so often to see if we really value Him? If we really love Him? Isn't that what He asked Peter (John 21:15–17)?

When He steps back, it's not always about us, it's about Him. If He feels like He's been put on the back burner of our lives — put aside because of busyness or cares — then He may step back to see if He is most important. It rekindles the fire of desire in us for Him. It's not so much quantity of time spent with Him, but quality. If we are constantly thinking of worries and cares, that means that even when we are with Him in prayer, we are not thinking of Him or putting Him first. We are putting our worries first and therefore giving them more value. What a predicament! We know He wants us to come to Him with our cares and fears. As we do this and lay them down at His feet, we make Him most important. If we would just think of His goodness when fear comes in, this will make Him more important than our worries. And it will also break the hold of fear and worry in us. A two-fer (at the price of one)!

Children love to play hide-and-seek. It teaches them that although they hide, we will always search for them, and that we will always find them. It teaches them confidence that we will never leave them. And it teaches them that when we hide, we will always be found. And when we are found, it gives the child joy. If the Lord hides from us for a while, we can be confident that He will always be found if we search for Him. We can be confident that He will never leave us. And when we find Him, there's more joy than before.

I remember when my husband Bill and I were first dating. He went away to college and I went to a college near my home. It was almost unbearable to be away from each other. Forty years later, I never tired of being with him because I knew what it was like being away from him. The Lord wants us to feel that way about Him, too. When my husband came home, we were closer than before. That's what happens with the Lord as well.

Sometimes our flame gets low because our oil starts running out. It happens for so many because they don't know how to continue to get closer to the Lord. For some that are very "new," they have not yet learned or been taught how to talk to the Lord, or have not been told that they can hear Him. God has not changed from the first time they felt His love, but they did not know what to do to nurture it, to keep the flame burning. Nurturing is the continual knowledge of God's love and care. It's different from that first revelation of His love. It's like when couples are first married. They are in love but haven't fully experienced love to the depths of couples that are married many years and have nurtured and cared for one another. It is a deeper revelation of that first love. We will have revelation of His love as we grow deeper in wisdom and knowledge of Him — and we do that by communication with Him.

Most of us desire to know Him more, to know more of His love. All we have to do is search our hearts. There may be times that we have to search deep, like when we don't feel His love. But when we search for Him, He will be found (Proverbs 8:17). In the ocean, the treasures are always deep and at the bottom. In the earth, the treasures are buried.

As we dig deeper, we will find the treasures of God's heart and love. They've been there all the time.

It takes two to tango! The Lord reaches out and reaches out, but we need to reach out to Him also. One can stretch out a hand, but unless the other moves to touch it, there is no hand holding. How do we nurture our relationship with the Lord? How do we nurture our relationship with our lover? We want to be with them and talk to them and find out what their heart's desire is. We want to please them and listen to what they have to say. We develop a relationship that begins with attraction love — that love that is a strong force that says, "this one is for me" and develops into an all-encompassing love that includes everything: attraction, steadfastness, nurturing. It's a love that is everlasting. It stays in good times and in bad.

Love is not just a feeling, although that's the way it is described. For there may be times when we don't "feel" God's love, yet it is always there — it is constant. There are times when we don't feel like our spouse loves us, such as during times of stress, misunderstanding, or hardship, but they still love us. It is the reason they are still with us. Love is the underlying cord that can't be broken. If this is so with human love, then how much more is it so with the love of God? People sometimes think that when they go through trouble or hard times that it is because God doesn't love them or doesn't love them as much as another. But He is no respecter of persons, nor does He change (Malachi 3:6). God loves us regardless of whether we think or feel that He does.

We should not measure the love of God by whether we are on the mountaintop or valley, for it is in the valley that God can do His greatest work in us. It is in the valley that He can help us grow. It is in the valley that He can draw us closer to Him and give us a greater understanding of Him — if we let Him and do not turn away. Valley experiences help us to withstand the mountaintop and not fall. For it is when you go from the valley to the mountaintop that you can look down and see where you've been — where you came from, and what you've learned. You can't appreciate the view if you've not been in the valley, and the rougher the climb, the greater the victory. We don't like valley experiences, but we can all look down from that mountaintop, knowing that we've learned from the experience, and we have a greater compassion for those still down there.

Love can be conceived for others (in us) in the valley and birthed on the mountaintop so that we can help those in need. It is only God that conceives that love for others in us, and how we know His love for us. We may not feel it in the valley, however, it's not only there for us, but it's there that His love is put in us for others as well. Isn't it amazing how we may not feel God's love for us at those times, yet it is in those very times when we don't feel it that He is actually putting in us more love for others?

We should not give up on the Lord when troubles come. We should not think He's failed us or stopped loving us. We should not separate ourselves from Him or "divorce" Him. It is at those times when the Lord will want to nurture us and sometimes we won't let Him. We may even blame Him instead.

In prayer one day, I saw an upside-down heart with the pointed part on the top and asked the Lord what He meant by it. He told me that an upside-down heart is steady: it doesn't topple easily, it is fixed. It is easy to pour into. It is pointed toward Him. When our hearts are fixed on Him, we know that all is well. Even if we get a bad report at the doctor, etc., we do not get mad at the Lord or think that He failed us. We simply fix our heart on Him and know that He will work it out and all will be well. We don't turn from Him, but instead hold onto His promises and Word. Our heart is fixed (Psalm 112:7), our faith is strong that the next report will be so good that we can give Him the glory. And if it isn't, we know that He is still in control. That's a heart He can pour into. Our faith makes us whole (Matthew 9:22). An upside-down heart is one that loves the Lord enough to let Him have His way. Love doesn't fail when it doesn't get what it wants. It is steady and secure in God's love for us, knowing that all will be well. It lets God work out what He has for us, trusting that what He has is what is best. It's because of that steadfastness that He can pour into it. An upside-down heart doesn't desire what *it* wants; it desires to do what the other wants. It seeks to give God the glory instead of self. It is becoming more Christ-like instead of flesh-like. It is an open vessel that God can pour His heart into. It receives from Him freely. It is open to Him at all times. And as it receives from the Lord, it pours out to others. It is a never-ending flow.

Heart spelled backwards is:

T—*To*
R—*Revere*
A—*And*
E—*Exalt*
H—*Him*

There is a hole in God's heart — it bleeds for His people that have distanced themselves from Him. He wants us to be His valentine. But instead of a fancy heart, He has given us His only Son and His love on the cross. One day in prayer, I saw Jesus take a cross necklace from around His neck and place it around mine. He told me that the cross is a symbol of His love for us. Many don't understand fully. You see, a lover gives his love a heart necklace or locket to symbolize and show his love. The cross symbolizes Jesus' heart, His love for us. But even more than that, it is His very life's blood that He shed for our life. He gave up His life for ours, because of His love for us. By giving up His life on earth, He will have us with Him forever. So the cross is more than a heart. He gave us every part of Him — all of Him — to have our love, and to have us with Him always. So when you see the cross, think of it as a heart — think of it as a symbol that He gave His all for you.

God is love. When we meet our mate on earth, we feel complete in our love for one another. When we meet the Lord, we are complete in our spiritual love. We become three-corded: Jesus, our spouse, and ourselves. Just as our love for our mate grows, so does our love for the Lord.

As each soul comes to Him, His heart is filled more and more. As each one accepts the Lord, His heart receives them. He has always loved them, but now that love is complete, not one-sided. There is nothing missing. There is nothing broken, for His heart breaks when His love is not returned. When His love is accepted and we return our love to Him, the piece that is missing is back. It's like a puzzle when a piece is missing, whether that missing piece is in a person or in God, it's incomplete. When it is found and put in place, it is whole. God wants all the pieces of His heart — all whom He loves — to be with Him. He wants none lost. Each one holds a special place that no one else can fill.

Many feel lost, not knowing where they "fit." Who will show them their place in His heart? People have to know where they fit in — what their purpose is and whom they are connected to. Otherwise they wander about trying to find something and they don't know what it is. They try this, they try that, and they even try what Satan has simply because they are looking to find their place, yet can't seem to find it. God has their proper fit in Him. Their place is waiting for them. If they try to find it somewhere else, it's uncomfortable. It can even hurt, like squeezing into a small shoe. When they find the proper fit, it's a relief to their body, mind, and soul, for all are connected.

As I was in prayer one day, I felt the Lord say the scripture in my spirit, "As the hart panteth after the water brooks, so panteth my soul after thee, O God" (Psalm 42:1). I told the Lord that was what I say to Him. He told me that those words are words that David echoed back to

Him. That He put those words in David's heart, for they are His heart. Love and desire are no good if they are one-sided. God desires us. He loves us.

We sometimes tend to think of the love relationship with God as being one-sided. However, just as not all scriptures are one-sided, neither is the love relationship. We receive His love, but we think that we do not have to do anything except receive. God needs to know of our love for Him, too. He wants us to show Him love, to give Him love. Sometimes people don't know how to do this. They come to church on Sunday wanting to learn how and what to do, and leave the same as they came. They leave empty. They are disappointed and frustrated because they want more. But they expect church to do it *for* them. The love relationship isn't a Sunday relationship. You can't get it all in one day a week. That's like dating on Saturday night and never getting married. And although those that have been Christians for a long time usually know the Lord more than newer believers, it is not always a hard and fast rule. It's not always about how *long* you've been a Christian. Every one is at different stages in their growth. Some newer Christians know the Lord more than some longtime Christians. The one who has spent one hour every day for twenty years talking to the Lord and having intimacy with Him, who has spent time with Him in the night watches, will know Him more than one who has one hour a week with the Lord on Sunday for forty years.

The love relationship is constant. It is a continual talking, being with each other every day. It is including each other in today and in the future. It is talking about the good things and figuring out how to handle the bad — together. It's like a marriage relationship that nurtures and grows into a deeper one; it's not a dating relationship. It's learning about each other, and not just looking to God when you want Him to meet a need in a crisis and then not talking to Him until the next one. The Lord wants to share our joys, too. He wants to share them as part of a relationship, not just looking from the outside. We want that closeness, that relationship, but so often just don't know how to reach out to Him and get it. It's no mystery, but we make it one. If we've failed in earthly relationships, we think it is impossible for us to have one with God. God wants us to not only know *how* to have that relationship, but that He is *waiting* for us, and *desiring* that relationship with us. He does not want us to be discouraged if it takes time for it to grow. Just as earthly relationships take time to grow, so does it take time for us to get to know the Lord. People who are married fifty years know a lot more about each other than when they first met! It is not different with the Lord. We tend to make it so complicated. All it takes is love — and God even gives us that love that we need!

God's love for us is unconditional. It's hard for us to understand that kind of love. People will fail, and if they do not understand God's unconditional love for them, they separate themselves from Him. This is especially true if they don't know or have never experienced unconditional love. They may have head knowledge, but until they have heart knowledge, they will never understand it. It's like when people know and can believe God will heal Jane but can't believe it for themselves. It's the same principle. They know they're not "good enough," or "lovable enough" when they fail. They won't or don't love themselves at that time, so, they reason, why would God? So they separate from Him or put up walls between God and them. They do it so that they "protect" themselves from being rejected and hurt. But that's how the flesh loves — human love. They equate the love they've experienced to the love of the Lord. God's heart aches for them. He loves them no matter what. It's true He doesn't like the sin, but He loves *them*. He forgives them. He still desires them. He still wants them. The only thing that separates them from God is their wrong assumption of Him and His love. He will not push them away, but they push Him away. They put up barriers. How can God's love penetrate unless they keep the door open to Him? He is always waiting for them, ready to forgive.

I thought about this and asked the Lord how we change wrong thinking when we don't even realize it? All it takes is a crack in the wall, the barrier — a hole in the dyke — for just one drop of love to seep in. Once it enters, the floodgates will break through. For some, the drop enters by hearing about God's love. For others, it is by God showing them His love in some way. For others, the Holy Spirit gives them a "knowing" in their spirit. Hearing comes for those that never knew of the Lord. Showing is for those that can't believe for themselves. Knowing, by the Holy Spirit, gives them revelation of God's love for them. All it takes is one drop of love to break down the walls of wrong mindsets. These walls are built of lies and wrong thinking from the enemy and from past experiences that he uses to convince and destroy. However, if a constant drop of water can wear away a stone, how much more can a drop of love wear away and break down wrong thinking!

God hasn't given up on us. He never has and never will. He loves us more than we can love ourselves. He gave His life for us because He loves us. Only that love can help us die to wrong thinking and mindsets. We may have head knowledge *of* His love, but when we can *feel* His love — when we experience His love and have a personal relationship with Him — that makes all the difference. For example, we can be attracted to someone and hear that they are attracted to us, but unless we get close to them and learn about them and care for them, we can never have intimacy. God does not want His people at a distance. He wants them close enough to hold them in His arms. Rainfall starts with one drop! (See Chapter 1 *Walking in the Spirit — There's Power in the Wind.*)

Just as the Lord gives us unconditional love, He loves it when we give Him unconditional love. We do this when, in times of testing, we seek Him and do not turn from Him. Then, as we pass the test and love

Him and look to Him in good times as well as hard times, He blesses us beyond measure. For when we love someone, the person that is loved unconditionally will give to us in return.

When Adam and Eve saw the apple, they desired it. It was pleasing to their eye. We are the apple of God's eye (Deuteronomy 32:10). That means we are His desire. He desires us. When we love someone, we desire them more than anything else. When we desire someone, we love them and want to make them happy. Because He loves us, because He desires us. He will give us our heart's desire, as long as that desire is good for us. He wants to do good things for us. He wants to bless us.

God wants His glory to not only cover and blanket the earth, but to be inside of it. He showed me a vision of the earth, but with a glass inside of it. He then started to explain what this meant. He wants people to know His love and wants His glory to surround them, but He also wants to be at the very core of their being. He wants to permeate every cell and fiber. He wants to fill them to overflowing with His love. He wants everyone to know the fullness of His love, the fullness of His power. No one missing, no one lacking. He wants the earth to be *filled* with His glory — not just surrounded, but *filled*. If a glass is surrounded by water on all sides except the top, it can still be empty. He wants all people to be partakers, not just watchers. Some are like the glass: They can see His Glory in others but feel empty themselves. Now is the time. He wants all to be filled. How does this happen? Eyes will be opened to His love for them, which will open their hearts. The heart is the "glass" so to speak. The earth is like the body, the glass is the heart. God's desire is that every person on earth would know His love and be filled with His Glory. Not just onlookers, but partakers.

We have all heard the story when we were children of "Goldilocks and the Three Bears." There were three beds, but only one was "just right." It always amazes me how God will teach me from something I have not thought about in years. He has shown me before about how a bed is a place of intimacy, but this time He was teaching me about our relationship with Papa, Jesus, and the Holy Spirit. Papa's bed is a place of security. It is a place of safety and protection. It is a place of nurturing love. We will never stop being His child therefore we can run to His bed whenever we need Him to wrap His arms around us.

Jesus' bed is a place of intimacy as we are His bride. It is a place of oneness where we reveal our hearts to Him and get to know His heart of love for us. It is a place where we can pour out the cry of our hearts to Him.

The Holy Spirit's bed is a place of comfort. It is also a place of instruction where we can come to learn. It is a bed of wisdom and guidance for our lives. It is a place where we can talk about the events in our lives and get direction. It's a place where we gently find out about wrong decisions, choices, and thinking so we can get up and move into all God has for us. It is a place of clarity where we can go whenever we need help. It is a place to get a gentle touch or a powerful revelation.

We will always be child, bride, and friend — regardless of the level of spiritual maturity we are at. With Goldilocks, only one bed was right. But with Papa's, Jesus', and the Holy Spirit's beds, each one is just right and at the right time for what we need.

Chapter 2

That Darn Apple!

Ever since Adam and Eve took the bite of the apple, we have been blaming each other and Satan has been having a field day with the results. Even though Jesus has done His part on the cross, we don't always realize or walk in the authority He has given us. And just as Satan twisted God's words to Adam and Eve, he is still doing the same with us today.

Blame is one of the tools the enemy uses against us to stop the blessing that is on its way. It's a spiritual "dam" to get us off track to focus on who's right or wrong instead of what is going on spiritually. Satan will use spiritual triggers that he knows will cause strife, anger, and blame. Issues from the past — subconscious or conscious — old hurts and wounds that have been buried deep inside. These may have been successful triggers in the past, so he can be pretty confident that it will work again. We should not fall into the trap of saying, "you made me feel this way," or "do that," for if we do, it will be exactly what Satan wants us to do. We have to resist the urge to justify ourselves so that we can understand what the Lord wants us to learn. If we do this, one of the enemy's weapons will be taken away. Show love for one another and don't let insignificant things block our blessings because of blame, anger, impatience, and hurts. Satan would laugh as he watches us fall into his traps and out of blessings. God wants to shower us with blessings. Don't let petty things get in the way. And don't take a bite of that apple!

Blame is looking for fault, shifting what is really from you to another. It is dangerous not to be able to admit when you're wrong. It's playing into the hands of the devil. Sometimes people are afraid to admit when they are wrong for fear that if someone sees that they made a mistake, they will think less of them. But it is not perfection that is wanted from a spouse or friend. It is simple kindness. Perfection doesn't produce love, caring and kindness does. You don't always have to be right for fear that if you're not, you'll lose their respect or love. That's the devil's lie. In fact, it's just the opposite! Showing you care is admitting when you hurt someone or lost your patience or temper with them. It shows that the person is more important than your pride. It shows that you trust their love for you. The spouse or friend who can admit wrongdoing is actually the stronger one. Strength isn't in your perfection, it's in your care.

Jesus died for our sins and all we have to do is admit them, repent, and run to Him for forgiveness. Why is it that people find it so hard to forgive one another? Is it because they have asked that person before and were rejected and not forgiven when asked? Is it because when they asked for forgiveness, they were given a lecture instead of love? Is it because when they asked for forgiveness, they were met with more anger? What if Jesus treated us that way? Who would ever come? How could a person be reconciled to God? Yet, isn't that what we do sometimes? Isn't that the way our flesh behaves? No wonder so many don't understand the love and forgiveness of our Lord when they have to beg for forgiveness and fear reactions from others when they do so. How we persecute one another! Jesus was persecuted for us — for love. Is it any wonder why Satan uses anger as a weapon of destruction? When the flesh rises, let love react. When the enemy rises, take up your sword. Throw water on the fire and put it out; living water brings life and not destruction.

We do not live in a perfect world. But when we have the love of Jesus, we see a person for who they are, not what we make them out to be. And we do not assume they did something to us because we associated what they did with what we may have experienced in the past with someone else. We should not blame them or jump to conclusions without first stepping back and seeing things from their point of view, or even from a neutral point of view. We should give them the benefit of the doubt because we *know* them. We look at them instead for the reason we liked them in the first place. We put aside the blame and see their good qualities.

I don't remember where I heard or read this story, but it was many years ago and it always stuck with me. It was about a man who felt he didn't love his wife anymore and was at the point of getting a divorce. As a last resort, he started to write down her good qualities. At first, he couldn't find a lot, but then he started to remember more and more until the list got so long he fell in love with her all over again! Wouldn't it be so much better if, when we get angry with someone or start to blame them, even if we feel justified in that anger, we could just try to see the other's point of view, or give them the benefit of the doubt, or at least start thinking about all the good qualities in that person?

I know that this works for me. I start looking at their good qualities and love takes over. Does it take discipline? Of course! We all want to "run with it" and be mad or feel sorry for ourselves. We all would like a "pity party" in the flesh. God's Word says fretting doesn't do us any good (Psalm 37:1–9). When we fight the enemy, we use God's sword. When we fight the flesh, we use God's love that He put in us, we use His strength, and we walk in His ways. We can do all things through Christ, which strengths us (Philippians 4:13).

The Lord loves us even when we get angry with Him, when we blame Him for things in our lives that He did not cause, even when we think the worst of Him. It is love that conquers all — all anger, all hurts, all injustices. He sees our tears. Anyone who is to become more Christ-like will endure what He endured and still have love. We may have to hold up many crosses, yet the weight makes us stronger. The Lord gives us strength beyond our physical measure.

Jesus gave us authority in His name. He has done His part on the cross. Now we need to walk in that authority that He has given us, instead of blaming Him when things go wrong. We need to take authority over the enemy and take dominion over what is ours. We need to pray with the authority that speaks faith. We need to ask, believe that we received, and take authority over it. Otherwise, Satan will just keep on taking. In *Lessons I Learned From The Lord,* I gave an example of how Satan is like a bully. We need to tell him to give it back and mean it! The violent take it by force (Matthew 11:12). Satan will not listen to wimps. When we ask in Jesus' name, according to God's will, He will give it to us. God, who has scheduled all things before we were born, who put the desire in us, has already given it to us. But the enemy snatches away what he can. He does it so craftily that we never think to blame him as the one who has done it. One reason Jesus died on the cross is for *sozo.* The Greek word *sozo* means salvation, but it's more than just forgiveness of sins. He gave us back the dominion and authority Adam lost when we use His name. If you want what the Lord already told you He has given you, take it back. The enemy has been allowed to keep our stuff because we haven't understood about dominion. My people are destroyed for lack of knowledge (Hosea 4:6).

The Lord wants to give us the desire of our hearts (Psalm 37:4). However, it's like when someone tries to give a baby a toy and the bully comes and snatches it away before the baby gets it in his hand. Baby Christians don't know how to get it back. They don't even know that they can have it because it never got into their hands. It was snatched away before they received it. Sometimes it is snatched away before they even see it. So many of us just know to ask. We wait, but we don't real-ize that we have to do something when we don't see it. Sometimes it has to do with God's timing. But too often it has been snatched away. We think God hasn't answered us and our faith fails. We even blame the Lord. (It's that apple thing again!) Daniel fasted and prayed for three weeks. God sent an angel to fight for him (Daniel 10). We should ask and pray until we know in our spirits that the Lord has released it to us. Then, if we don't receive it, we need to take dominion over it. When God opens a door, if it stalls, take dominion. We will sense it in our spirit when we need to do this. Satan will steal, and then he will try to make us think that God said "no." He'll try to get us to fear, or to lose faith in the Lord, or even to be mad at Him. He works with the flesh — human nature. For example, suppose we asked a friend for something and they said "yes." They put what we asked for by our front door, but then someone stole it. We never knew they delivered it, so we become mad at them. We blamed them and thought they had broken their promise. What we need to do is get it back from whoever stole it from us.

Sometimes God's promises to us are so big that the enemy will try his very best to prevent them, but he can't win unless we give up. All it takes is for us to walk in the authority that Jesus gave us and take back our stuff. You see, in the case with the bully, when the daddy steps in and tells the bully to give it back, the bully is small compared to the daddy, and he is intimidated by him. When we use the name of Jesus, the bully shrinks and is intimidated. He fears. Use the name of Jesus with authority. It's powerful!

How many times have we blamed the Lord for what the enemy did to us? And how many times have we blamed someone for thinking negatively of us when that wasn't the intention at all? I wonder how the Lord feels when we assume He thinks negatively of us, especially be-cause He loves us so much? How it must hurt Him. And I wonder how our spouse or friend must feel when we assume they think negatively of us? Just as we don't understand the height and depth and breadth of God's love for us, we don't always understand others' love for us either.

We all need to have more love for others, and every one of us needs more love. There was a television program on several years ago called *The Love Boat*. In those stories, there would always be problems. Problems we have can sometimes "rock the boat" and make the waters rough, but God can always turn the problems for our good. In fact, the rocking boat can cause the problems to fall overboard to get rid of them. By the time the boat comes into port, all is well. Sometimes the rough seas in marriage are there to expose the problems so that they can be dealt with and gotten rid of, resulting in a happy ending. But for this to occur, the marriage has to have God as the anchor. It has to be three-corded, both husband and wife entwined to the Lord so that it doesn't break apart. A well-oiled cord can't have garbage hanging onto it. So as the junk is brought to the outside of us, it slides off and it is removed. The boat may rock once in a while, but it is so the bad stuff goes overboard and is gotten rid of. The rope may have a bit of junk trapped inside, but as it works its way out, it slides off. What we go through, any struggles, misunderstandings, anger, or annoyances with one another, happens to expose and get rid of the garbage. We should not jump overboard with it, but hang on and trust God to handle it. Then we will become stronger and there will be more room for love as the garbage is removed. If we stick it out, we can look back and see that God does work everything for our good, as long as we make Him a cord in the equation. Instead of arguing and blaming each other, we will have more understanding. It isn't always easy, because of…

That darn apple!

Chapter 3

Calling All Crooners

Praise and worship is when our desire is *for* Him and not *from* Him. Praise is **P**resenting **R**eal **A**ppreciation **I**n **S**ong for **Ev**erything. Worship is **W**hen we **O**ffer and **R**elease our **S**pirit **H**igher **I**n **P**raise.

There is an expression that when someone has a great love for another, they "worship" the ground that they walk on. Worship is love in its greatest form. It is adoration — the "love is blind" thing that only sees perfection in the person. It's when their world revolves around that person. It's when their thoughts are always on that person, no matter what they are doing. It is being consumed with love for them. When we worship the Lord, it is that all-encompassing love that no words can describe. Yet, His love for us is even greater than that. It is more than human love can understand. It is a love that overlooks our faults and sees the good. It is a love that sees what we *can* be and not what we *are*.

Worship is an *act* resulting from great love. Love is what we *feel*; worship is what we *do* because we feel. It is a natural expression of love. It is singing, dancing, clapping, and raising our hands. It is pure joy. And it is freedom to express that joy. If people are exuberant with love and joy, how can they not clap? Or raise their hands to heaven? Or shout? Or sing? These are natural expressions of joy. At a ball game, people shout and clap when someone scores. They express it. In fact, they can't contain it. Why do God's people sit in church with no expressions of joy? Paul sang bound in chains and was freed. Praise breaks the chains. Even if we don't realize it, praise is for *our* good. God doesn't need praise. But when we praise Him, our chains fall off. The enemy flees. It is freedom. Why do so many of us sit silently in our misery? Even if we don't feel like it at first, if we sing or speak words of praise, after a while, it will refresh our spirits. It is not easy, but it will work if we don't give up.

Praise and worship is expressing our love for the Lord, but as praise rises, it comes back as refreshing to us. What goes up, must come down! The fastest way to get out of a pit (depression) is to raise our hands to be lifted out. When we raise our hands in praise, the Lord will lift us out. Those that choose to stay in the pit, have a "pit-y" party. They sometimes want others to share in their misery. But if someone is drowning in quicksand, you don't jump in with them; you throw them a rope and pull them out. But only if they raise a hand to grab it.

The Lord loves children. Is it any wonder? They have such freedom as they sing love songs to the Lord. It's only when we get older and more "mature" that we develop inhibitions about showing our emotions as we worship the Lord. It is then that we get heavy-handed. Come on, you know what I'm talking about: It becomes hard for us to raise our hands in praise. It's like the enemy is sitting on them! If we feel courageous, we might raise a hand up quickly, so that no one will notice. I remember one Sunday in church, seeing a young boy just dancing and singing before the Lord. He reminded me of how it must have been with King David. What freedom! May we learn to be like children again in our praises, worshipping Him in spirit and in truth. Isn't that how little children do it?

I had a smokestack come to mind in prayer one day. It had white smoke billowing out. I got the impression that you can't see the smoke unless the air is cold outside and the warm air hits it, like people's breath in the cold air. Worship warms the atmosphere. It changes it because of love. Love warms cold hearts and changes them. When we worship the Lord, we change the atmosphere and miracles happen. The Holy Spirit moves in an atmosphere of love and warmth.

Worship is when our spirit is in harmony with the Lord's. Worries and fears disappear. Ears open and there is more clarity in hearing Him at that time. Wisdom and revelation enter in. Praise and worship opens and unlocks the door. Harmony is a word used in music. It is a musical agreement of sounds. Each is a separate tone, but coming together in unison, it is so much better. It is so much better when our spirit is in harmony with the Lord's as we worship Him.

When we sing from our heart, it makes no difference what we sound like out of our mouths, for God hears what comes from our hearts. It is as if the music is coming right out of our heart. So those of us who are embarrassed because we can't hold a tune should sing anyway. It's music to His ears.

Singing lifts our spirit. I think of a song simply called "Sing" that my children used to like to hear on *Sesame Street* and sing many years ago. The words were (although I'm not sure I'm remembering them exactly): "Sing, sing a song, sing out loud, sing out strong. Sing of good things, not bad. Sing of happy, not sad." It always lifted my spirit when I heard that song. It's hard to stay depressed when we sing. It is also hard to sing when we are depressed. But if we press through and put on a song, depression will break. Our spirit will come in harmony with the song. That is why it is dangerous for teens to listen to music that has demonic undertones or negative, depressing, suicidal words. That is what their spirit will come in harmony with. They don't even realize it. Be careful what enters your ears: Satan enters through the senses. Don't give him the key to come in.

Praise and worship are also our weapons in fighting the enemy.

He cannot stand by and hear us praise the Lord. Sometimes when we are in battle, and the battle is going on for a long while, we may feel like we are stretched to the breaking point and we have no more strength in us to fight any longer. It's so hard to get up the energy we need. I was feeling exactly like this when God reminded me of Moses. When he was so tired during the battle that he could not hold up his arms any longer, his two friends held them up for him (Exodus 17:12). Praise and worship are those friends. In fact, even though it may take an effort to start to praise, we will get to a point — if we do not give up — where the praise is energizing us and giving us strength and joy. (It also helps to have two good friends in the Lord that we can call on to lift us up.) Three cords are not easily broken.

It is also a sacrifice when we take time to praise the Lord. When we sing praise songs, we are thinking of the Lord and blessing Him for His goodness to us. It pleases Him that we remember to thank Him for all He's done.

We can feel the Holy Spirit's presence right from the start of praise. But worship — the "I love you" songs — brings us deeper into His presence and ushers in the *move* of the Holy Spirit. It's when He takes over the service and we *know* He's about to do something special. We can *feel* His power. His power is there to heal and deliver. It's when miracles happen. Sometimes we stop just short of the move of the Holy Spirit.

Praise stems from a thankful heart. We can thank the Lord in so many ways: by obeying Him, having faith in Him, encouraging others, and letting His light shine from us. And one of the ways is praise!

The family that prays and praise together, stays together.

Chapter 4

The Father's Love

One day, a while ago, as I was praying, I heard the Lord say, "Why don't you ever call me Father? You usually just say God, and I want you to see Me as Father." I asked the Lord's forgiveness and asked Him to help me to see Him as Father, Daddy, Papa. I then asked Him if He were trying to teach me something. He said He wanted me to see the love relationship between Father and child. It's more intimate than God and child. He told me that I've seen His love as Jesus, now He wants me to see His love as Father God, Papa, Daddy. Jesus loves us as His bride; Father God loves us as His child. His love is three-corded: Father, Son Jesus, and Holy Spirit. Now He wanted me to see in my heart the love of the Father. One love, three facets. When we understand each, we understand *complete* love. I had previously read the very moving writing, *The Father's Love Letter*, and I've seen and felt this love of the Father, but I still thought of His love in terms of God, not Father. God wants to bring us to revelation of Himself as Father, not just God. It's like a child calling their father "sir" instead of daddy. The child knows the father loves him, but there's a formality, not intimacy. Father is the next step, but Daddy or Papa is the most intimate, close, heart-felt knowledge of His love.

Love for a child is instinct. Even most animals take care of their babies. Yet it is the Father's love — God's love — that is known to all mankind. Even before someone comes to know Father personally, each has the instinctive knowledge of love for a child. If a worldly father can want to take care of his child, how much more so will our Heavenly Father?

Papa wants us to know that He has a special place in His heart for each one of us. As we seek Him and put Him first, then when we call upon Him, He will answer. Just as parents will drop what they are doing to come to their child's aid because the child is most important, Papa wants us to realize that is exactly what He does when we call. We are important to Him. He wants us to *know* this with such assurance that we never doubt that He will answer; there will be no question about it. He will *always* come when we call to Him. Isaiah 49:16 says, "Behold, I have graven thee upon the palms of *my* hands; thy wails *are* continually before me." He loves us.

Children have such faith. They love fairytales, and like in Peter Pan, they say, "I believe, I believe." They know it's just pretend, yet they get so immersed in it, they believe. We all remember as children "wishing on a star' and believing our dreams would come true. That is childlike faith, that we will have the desires of our hearts. As adults, we have faith in God. He gives us the desires of our hearts (Psalm 37:4). He makes our dreams come true, for the desires and dreams we have are what He has put there. It's all in a word: magic is what the world wants. Miracles are what the Lord *does*. Believe in Miracles. What He does is real, yet people are afraid to believe. He does the impossible.

Papa wants us to come to Him with our needs and believe that He will answer. Yet so many times, we don't come to Him because we think we've asked Him for too many things. Sometimes it's because we don't want Him to think that we only come to Him for what He can do for us. We want Him to know that we love Him for Who He is, not for what He can do. He knows how we feel. That's why His Word says in Isaiah 43:22, "But thou hast not called upon me, O Jacob; but thou hast been weary of me, O Israel." He would not tell us to ask if He would not answer. This does not mean His answer will always be in the exact way we want it to be, but He will always answer. He says in Isaiah 45:19, "I have not spoken in secret, in a dark place of the earth: I said not unto the seed of Jacob, Seek ye me in vain: I the Lord speak righteousness, I declare things that are right." I have found that He does even more than what I expected, or in a better way. We should not think of Him as a "fairy godfather" just to grant requests. However, we should know that as we give our hearts to Him, we can ask Him for anything, even the impossible, for He does miracles, not magic, and what He does is real. Have faith in God. Let's not forget the little child in us. There is nothing as precious as a child's unconditional love. Believe as a child, love Him unconditionally as a child — and our lives will be full of miracles!

It is the Father's love for His people that brought them out of slavery. It is His love for them that protected their first-born sons (Exodus). It is because of His love for us that He gave His Son's life for ours. It was for love. If He did all this for love, then anything we ask, won't He also do? It is by knowing this and walking in this knowledge that gives victory. Live expecting the Father's goodness. Don't even question it. Expect to be in health. Expect prosperity. Double-mindedness is from the enemy. Thinking He will heal someone else and not us is telling the Lord you don't believe He loves you. It is rejecting what He wants to give us and it's rejecting His love. What if we wanted to give someone a gift and the person refused it, saying that we really want someone else to have it, and that we love that other person more? Why is it that we are so afraid that Father will disappoint us that we refuse to believe He wants to give to us? Are we so used to being disappointed in the world that we carry it over to our Heavenly Father?

When we give Papa the desires of our hearts, we put our heart in His hands and we trust Him with it. He will not let our heart be broken. Psalm 37:3-5 states, "Trust in the Lord, and do good; so shalt thou dwell in the land, and verily thou shalt be fed. Delight thyself also in the Lord; and he shall give thee the desires of thine heart. Commit thy way unto the Lord; trust also in him; and he shall bring it to pass." Even the secret desires — the unspoken ones, the ones deep in our hearts — He knows every one and takes care of each. He knows that these mean more to us than the surface ones we so easily talk about.

Papa wants us to dream big. To a child, a small toy boat in a bathtub can seem just like a boat in the ocean. He imagines it. To an adult, the ocean is a huge body of water. But to the Lord, the ocean is just a small speck in the universe. We need to think big, dream big, imagine big. For our biggest dreams are very small to the Lord. Nothing is impossible to Him.

Just recently, as I was seeing some of the promises God had given me start to come about, I was full of anticipation to see them fully completed. As I was asking Papa how He was feeling, I felt Him say that He was full of anticipation, too. When we are tuned in to each other, we can sense what God is feeling. He was excited and anticipating giving me these good things, for it gives Him pleasure to give to His children. I thought of the old ketchup commercial that focused on anticipation. He anticipates giving, and we anticipate receiving. It's like that with our children also. We love to give to them; therefore, we anticipate being able to give them a gift, and they anticipate receiving it from us!

Our heavenly Father owns everything. He always has and He always will. But when we walk with Him, we are one — we are connected. Because we are one with Him, He gives us all He has. I remember when my husband Bill and I were first married. He brought with him a blanket that he had in college, and because we were young and did not have very much, we used it on our bed. He used to tease me about it being *his* blanket when I took a little too much of it on my side, since he had owned it before we were married. Of course, he felt everything we had was ours, but he still liked to tease me by saying he owned it before we were together. When we give ourselves to the Lord, we become one with Him, and all He has is ours also.

Papa wants to give us His joy, His peace, His happiness. His joy brings health. The Word of God says that a merry heart does much good like a medicine (Proverbs 17:22). We need to just *expect* good things. Not that we try to have more faith. Papa gives us faith. So it doesn't take great faith on our part — just *great expectations!* When we know someone loves us, we expect good things from them. Do we really know that Papa loves us? It's not pride or arrogance to expect Papa to do good for us. It's confidence in His love for us. That pleases Papa. I'm not talking about being greedy or "spoiled" here, but knowing Papa's love and walking in that love. And because of His love, when He meets our needs, we can help meet others' needs. It's the "love cycle."

When you know His love, you don't doubt or have greed
You just expect Him to meet every need
You receive what He gives, and then you share
That others will see your love and care
It's a cycle of love that began with His Son
He gave us His all — the battle's been won
So when you remember His Son on the tree
Believe that He did it because He loves thee

Love wants what is best for the other. Papa wants His best for us. We are the ones that limit ourselves. We do this by wrong thinking, controlling mindsets, fear, labels that others have placed upon us that we accept as truth. How Papa must just want to nudge us along and tell us to be all that He's made us to be! As a parent, I want what is best for my children, not what is best for me, because I love them. I want them to be free to be all that they can be, to accomplish all that Papa has for them, regardless of where He takes them. I want them to trust the Father's love and His care of them. I am reminded of the story in the Bible about King Solomon and his wisdom in dealing with the two women who each claimed the one baby as theirs. The real mother — the one who truly loved her child — was willing to give him up so that he would be safe and be able to grow up to be all that God made him to be, even if it meant him being taken away from her (1 Kings 3:16–27).

My heart goes out to birth mothers having to give up their babies for adoption. How heart-wrenching it must be for them to give them up; yet, they love that child so much that they place that child in a home that can provide what they cannot. If this is true of human parents, that they want their child to have the best in life, how much more does Papa want His children to be all that they can be and to have all that He has for them? We limit ourselves. God doesn't limit us. So often we are taught as Christians not to limit God, but you see, God doesn't limit us either! Limitations aren't one-sided. We can either go by our own thinking or reasoning, which will limit us, or we can believe that with God, all things are possible. Even a shining star, when placed in a box, can't shine. When we open our minds to what Papa has for us, we see unlimited possibilities. Papa will open doors for us, but an open door is only good if we walk through it. Get out of the box and start shining!

God has so much more for us than we can see for ourselves. Yes, He may ask us to do something we think we are not capable of doing, or go places we may not want to go. But if we say "yes" and obey, not grudgingly or complaining, we'll see the good He has planned for us. We can't see the end, but Papa does. He has good things in store for us when we say "yes."

How often do we murmur and complain when Papa is actually blessing us? We are just like the Israelites when God blessed them and took them out of slavery in Egypt so that they could be brought into the

Promised Land. They murmured and complained even after seeing God do miracles for them to get them out of slavery and bless them! As a result, they had to go around and around in the desert. They still didn't learn, however, but kept grumbling so that not one of the generation that left Egypt got into the good land. How often does Papa bless us, yet we don't see the good that He's doing. We don't look ahead and trust His plans for us, so we grumble and complain because it's not exactly the way we thought it should be. Or we complain that to get to the blessing we may have to do something we don't want or like to do. What spoiled children we can be! Yet He still loves us and is good and kind and patient to us as we learn. Some of us may never learn, which may sadly result in us not coming into all Papa has for us. We need to trust that God does work *all* things for our good (Romans 8:28). He knows our emotions and He knows what we may be feeling. But I wonder if, when we take it to the extreme in our grumbling and complaining, we are not doing Him a disservice and making Him sad, when He just wants to give us this blessing. I've had to ask for forgiveness many times because I did not see the big picture of what Papa was doing for me. I can now look back at what my husband and I thought was a bad time in our lives only to realize that we could not have come into all God had for us if we did not go through it. I'm so thankful He loves me in spite of my ignorance.

One day I was pushing my little granddaughter on a swing. She kept asking me to push her higher, and I kept telling her to hold on tight. The Lord used that to teach me how He wants to push us higher. He wants us to hold onto Him tight. As He takes us to new heights, He is right behind us — guarding us, watching us, and having fun with us. When children swing higher and higher, they have fun. The higher they go, the more fun it is for them. It is adventure and excitement to them. Papa wants us to be as children, letting Him take us higher, and enjoying the adventure and excitement of it. We should not be afraid, for He is right there, and will not let us fall.

A young child doesn't limit his daddy. He hasn't learned about limitations; he only learns limitations as he grows older. It is the opposite in the spirit. Once we grow in the natural, we have to *unlearn* what we've learned about limitations with our Heavenly Papa. We have to learn to unlimit Him. As a child, we learn as we grow older that our natural father has limitations; we have to learn that our Heavenly Father does not. It goes against everything we've come to know. That's one reason we have to become as a child (Matthew 18:3–4). It is a re-birth of new thinking, new ways, and new attitudes; the old ways go and the new comes. It can't be done by our own willpower, but by the Holy Spirit. Once we give the Holy Spirit control, the limitations come off, the chains break off, and we can swing high. It has to do with trusting in Papa's love and care. A child trusts his daddy pushing him on the swing. He can relax and go higher and enjoy the ride, because his daddy is right behind him. He knows his daddy loves him and will see to it that he doesn't get hurt. When will we trust our Papa's love for us enough to let Him bring us higher? When will we trust Him to take us into all He has for us? Some of us are like the child who won't take his feet off the ground, dragging them to slow the swing down and never getting to that place of trust that brings freedom. How Papa longs for His children to stop dragging their feet and trust Him for all He has for them. It's as if the doors to their hearts have chains on them. They peek out through the opening but won't let Him in all the way. They shut the door quickly if He asks them to step out. What they don't understand is that the door of their heart has to open first, and if they let Him in, then they *and* Papa can step out into what He has for them, *together*. Do you trust the Lord enough to open the door of your heart wide?

We can't walk on water unless we get out of the boat. The boat is a place of comfort and safety. Yet it is a place where there is no change. It's easy to remain comfortable and hard to step out. Papa wants us to trust Him enough to step out. He coaxes us as a parent coaxes a baby to take his first steps. It may be a little scary, but He holds out His hand to us. He wants us to walk into all He has for us. He waits. He wants us to be flexible, to keep an open mind, and step into what He has waiting for us. He does not want us to be stuck in the muck of our own mind-set — limited in how we see our future. The muck is like quicksand, keeping us down and bound.

Papa reminded me of when we built our house many years ago. We went to see how it was coming along, and as my husband walked around the house, his foot got stuck in the mud and he lost his shoe. That shoe is still underground. How do *we* get out of the mud? The joy of the Lord gives us strength (Nehemiah 8:10). It has to do with our attitudes. Bad attitudes — grumbling and complaining — make us sink deeper. God's Word tells us to rejoice in trials (Romans 5:3). This is not easy, and I have to admit that I have to remind myself of this when going through a trial. But I think that favor comes to us when we give Papa thanks in all things. We can't help getting His blessings and favor then. It's easy to give thanks in good times. God pulls our feet out of the mud when we thank Him and appreciate Him in hard times, too. We can always find something that is not the way we want it, but that kind of mindset will sink us deeper. How about looking at our blessings instead? All things are possible with the Lord (Matthew 19:26). The water's fine; come on in!

Papa is our coach as well as our biggest fan. He loves us so much that He wants to teach us and coach us so that He can work out His plans for us. But how many of us really want to listen, or even want to hear His instruction? Some of us are either afraid of change, or are not willing to do what it takes to bring about change. Some of us don't want to admit there are things that need changing. How Papa wants the best for His children! He wants to bless each one of us. However, He can't work in us if we won't allow Him. He can't give us what we don't want for ourselves. But Papa is patient and waits for us. He will never give up on us. How we must exasperate Him sometimes just like Eliza Doolittle exasperated Professor Higgins in *My Fair Lady*. We are His fair "lady" and He wants to take us from caterpillar to butterfly. He wants us to be all that we can be. I know that I want to be an open vessel to hear my Coach at all times, because Papa can work with an open vessel, but He cannot pour into a closed one.

One day, I heard Papa tell me that I give Him joy. Then Papa said that He would also tell me that when we give Him joy, His Spirit is also lifted. He dances and sings over us because we make Him happy. God's Word says that the joy of the Lord is *our* strength (Nehemiah 8:10). So I wanted to know what *we* do when we give Him joy? We tend to think that scripture, and others, are just one-sided. We think in terms of what Papa can give us, not what we can give Him. It's true He owns the cattle on a thousand hills. He owns everything. But we can give Him joy, love, obedience, and happiness. Those are the gifts we can give Him. We want to obey Him because we love Him and because of what He did for us. That's what it's all about — love. People may follow laws grudgingly. But they obey the Lord and want to please Him out of love. For example, we pay our taxes because it's the law. We pay our tithes because we love Him. We obey the government out of duty. We obey the Lord out of love. We are no longer under the law like the Israelites, but under His love. Love sets the captives free.

Some parents have children that give them joy, and some parents have children that give them sadness. There are those children who are pessimists, always seeing the negative side of everything. And there are those who are optimists, always joyful and seeing the good in things and the possibilities. The Lord wants us to trust Him and have joy; He doesn't want us to worry. A child who is always worried and serious concerns his parents. But a child who is happy and has joy all the time, makes his parents happy. They know that the child trusts them to take care of everything. Faith is when we believe that God *can* take care of it. Trust is when we know that God *will* do it for *us*.

How it makes Papa sad when we are burdened and unhappy. One day, as I was going through a trial that weighed heavily on me, I sensed the Lord was solemn. I felt Him saying that He wants us to be happy and have joy. It makes Him sad when we are burdened.

Emotions are our choice. Just as love and anger are choices, joy is also a choice. It is a state of mind. Since the Lord is in us, when we are sad, so is He. When a parent who has joy sees one of their children is sad, because they love the child their joy goes. There is no joy in seeing a sad child. The child has a choice, and then the parent reacts to that choice. They are affected by it. One person's choice affects those who love them. Burdens and worries are like boxes or cans that are tied to us with strings. It's similar to when people tie tin cans to a car when a couple marries. We become married to our burden. Cut the strings and be free! Even if for no other reason than to make the Lord happy, I choose joy. And an added bonus is that laughter and joy are like "bug repellents" to keep the enemy's pesky flies away.

Papa has a sense of humor. He likes to laugh, too. We think of Him in such strange ways. Shouldn't He like laughter just as we do, since He made us in His image? Sin is not in Him, but He has joys and sorrows, just as we do. As stated earlier, God's Word says a merry heart does much good (Proverbs 17:22). He created everything, even laughter. He likes to have fun, too!

He is our Father — the Father of all. Sometimes we make Him happy, and sometimes we make Him sad, but He loves us at all times. He waits for the prodigals with open arms. He is patient with the rebellious ones. He loves us even when we fail. Isn't that what love is? This is especially true of a parent's love for a child. It's called unconditional love. The only thing that can separate us from Papa is us not wanting Him. He will always love us and want us. Nothing can change that. In

Isaiah 49:15, it states, "Can a woman forget her sucking child, that she should not have compassion on the son of her womb? yea, they may forget, yet will I not forget thee." The children that please Him and love Him with all their hearts, they lift His Spirit and give Him joy.

Papa is love. When we look at Him, we see love. We are His very own and He has created and chosen us from before time began. There is nothing that can change His love for us. He will never leave us. There may have been times when we felt He did not love us, but that was our own emotions, our own perceptions. Perceptions are not always truth. His Word is truth. He is love (1 John 4:8). Not as the world sees love, and not even as human parents see love. For even parents' love is affected by their own perceptions, emotions, and traditions. Papa's love does not turn on and off like a faucet. He does not "fall out of love," as the flesh does. His love does not go by sight, or touch, or any of the human senses. His love is all-encompassing, never-ending. Humans can't perceive it because they can only relate love to what they know. But there will come a time when everyone will shed their earthly bodies and emotions and know the extent of His love, and we will be able to love in the spirit. We will know love with no bounds. It will be pure joy. Earthly love can only be what people perceive. When two people meet and fall in love, they love who they perceive the person is. Love is blind, as the saying goes. But what happens when that perception changes? We can perceive all the good in a person, or all the bad. If only we could shut out the bad perception and remember what we loved in the beginning, and then speak what we love about them! What we see is what we get. Perceive the good and speak it to the person and see what happens.

Papa knows that we try so hard to please Him and feel so bad when we don't. However, He sees the intent of our hearts. We should never be afraid. He will always love us. His heart is an open book; it is written in the Bible. Every time we read it, we read what is in His heart.

He knows our hearts even better than we do. We never have to fear and wonder if He knows what we meant, or if He understands how we feel. He knows the intent of our hearts, for He made them. If He knows what we are going to say before we say it (Psalm 139), then surely He knows what we are trying to say even if we can't communicate it correctly. So we never have to fear that the Lord has misunderstood what we said. Fear does not come from the Lord. When we know Him more, we will become *fearless*.

As a parent, and now a grandparent, I've watched my children grow and mature into adults. Papa watches us as we grow and mature in spirit. I got the impression of Papa pushing me in a baby carriage, then holding me in His arms: I was a baby looking in His eyes and grabbing His finger as babies do, completely dependent on Him. Then I saw myself as a toddler, holding His Hand, walking by His side. Then I saw myself as a child, dancing with Him, my feet on top of His. Then I saw myself as an adult, walking side by side, but still holding His Hand as He taught me and gave me wisdom. Regardless of our age, naturally or spiritually, we need to look in His eyes and hold His Hand and be completely dependent on Him. At first, as babies we can't even feed ourselves, but then even as adults, even when we can feed ourselves, we get our nourishment from Him. As we listen to Him, as we read His Word, it is bread, life — nourishment. Regardless of our age, we are always His child. He cares for us, yet He doesn't control us, for He gave us free will. If we stray like the prodigal son, He will always welcome us home.

Papa waits for His children to come to Him. We are welcome to come at any time and sit right on His knee. Just as an earthly parent's door is always open to a child, so is Papa's house open to us. In fact, He waits in anticipation. He watches for us to come and be with Him. The father of the prodigal son watched for his child to come home, just as our heavenly Papa watches for His children to come home (Luke

15:11–32). He waits for each one. He loves us all. Nothing we do could ever stop Him from loving us. We may remove ourselves from Him, but He will never remove His love from us. We are, and always will be, His child. He is, and always will be Papa. He is the Father of Love.

Chapter 5

Love Talk, Or Not?

The Lord loves to be with us and enjoy us. Sometimes we get so busy with everyday activities that we don't take time to just *be* with Him. Sometimes we have so many problems and burdens that when we do take the time to talk with Him, it's to list our needs and complain about our problems. He wants us to come to Him with our burdens, but He also loves it when we seek Him to just enjoy being with Him. Has it been a while since you just "love talked" with Him? Has it been a while since you've taken the time to refresh yourself in Him? He is all around us. We can hear Him in the garden, or by the ocean. We can hear Him and be close to Him as we relax in His Presence. Think of Him as we stroll outside. Talk to Him and listen.

When spring comes, the air is clean and clear. There are times when we need to do "spring cleaning" of our minds, and clean and clear out the clutter. Just as our garages accumulate unnecessary junk, so can our minds. We need to take time from the busyness. Then He can tell us of the good things He has in store for us. He wants us to rest in Him and with Him. We don't have to talk about profound things. Just being and enjoying each other. That is when hopes and dreams come about. We usually have the most fun with our spouses when we are not doing work, but just enjoying and having the time to relax and really talk to each other, like when we are on vacation. Love talk comes from deep within the heart. Yes, there is a time for serious prayer-talk and intercession for others. But we also can't forget about our dream-talk with the Lord.

Isn't this what we love to do with our mates, dream about our future together? That usually is not a problem BK — before kids! But it is so important for parents to take time for themselves and have a date night. If we don't take the time to dream of the future together, if we don't love talk, when the time comes when it is again just the two of us, we'll have nothing to say. Love talk keeps the husband and wife relationship close. It's important to be together alone.

It's also just as important for us to be with the Lord alone and to love talk with Him. It keeps us close to Him. Time out from work is more important than people think. Time out from children is more important than people think. Time together alone and apart from others will nurture and freshen the relationship. It keeps it alive. It is the fuel that keeps your spirit, your love, as well as your body, going. It sustains it through times of business as usual. Sometimes this is what happens between us and the Lord. It's all work. We talk to Him of only problems and needs. God wants to love talk with us. He wants us to dream about our future together with Him in heaven and being with Him forever.

The Lord hears us whenever we talk to Him. But those that only seek Him in times of crisis sometimes have trouble finding the way to Him. It's not that He's not there, they just don't know how to get to Him. It's like when you go to a house that you've been to every day; you find it easily. But when you have not been there in a long time, you are not sure how to get there.

Love talk with our mate means listening to what the other has to say. When we listen to the other person, it says that we value that person, and that person is important to us, therefore what the person says is important to us. When we shut the door to communication, we also shut the door to intimacy. If we say that we are not interested in what the other has to say, we are rejecting the very heart of that person. It says to the person, you don't matter. What the subject matter is about is not the issue. It's the person's worth that is affected. One part of the love relationship is about listening. It's about valuing the other. Love is kind and does not tear down. It says: I care about you; therefore, I care about what you have to say. I may not care about what a stranger says, and I have the "right" not to listen to them, but I love you, and therefore, because I love you, because I care and value you, I *want* to hear about what is on your mind and what you have learned that day, even if *I* already know it. When we love someone, it is not about us, it's about them.

If a spouse isn't allowed to speak, sooner or later they will close their mouth but also their heart to you. Listening is a small price to pay for love. Wake up! How many marriages are shattered because a spouse is flattered by someone listening to them and making them feel like they have worth? It is not physical intimacy that may be lacking, but simple communication. Telling someone that you are not interested in what she has to say is the same as telling her that you are not interested in *her*. It is your right, but is the loss of love worth it? How would you feel if the shoe were on the other foot? Would you find someone else to open your heart to? The subject matter could be ordinary or even boring, but the love relationship listens as if it is hearing something from a V.I.P. You see, it's not *what* the person is saying but the *person* saying it that matters. A spouse who is listened to feels valued and therefore will value their spouse because they make them feel special.

Jesus is always interested in what His bride has to say. He will listen as if we are the most important one to Him. In fact, He wants us to talk to Him more. He cherishes us. Are we interested enough to listen to Him?

One day in prayer, I "saw" jam on a piece of crusty bread. I asked the Lord what He wanted to teach me. It was about speaking the truth in love. If we have two jams and no bread, nothing can hold it up. If we have two crusty breads and no jam, it's dry and tasteless. We need to have the toast to support the jam. We need its toughness and crustiness to hold it up. We need the sweetness of the jam so the bread is easier to eat. At times we need that toughness along with the sweet to speak the truth to others. The truth is not always easy to digest. It takes longer to digest crusty bread than jam. It has to be chewed on a little longer. But if we give people time, they will be able to digest it, and they will be able to see the jam (love) that went with it.

Sometimes love talk gets put on the "back burner" when we get so focused on work. It's not that we don't love our spouses, but our minds are not on love at that time. If that happens for too long a time, we get out of the "practice" of love. It's like when an elastic band remains stretched tight for too long a time, it wears out and can't relax back. It remains stretched out. When it's all work all the time, we get "strung out" and our nerves are shot. We forget how to relax and enjoy one another. When an elastic band is stretched too long, there's no "play" left in it. To keep the "spring" in your lives, your health, and your marriage, make sure you keep the play in it. Learn to laugh, even in situations that could cause you to be annoyed. Take the laugh path instead. It will be health to your navel (have a good belly laugh) and marrow to your bones. A merry heart does good (Proverbs 17:22), and since the heart keeps the rest of the body functioning, it's important to find joy and laughter. Look for it as you would a treasure. My grandmother lived to be 102 years old, and even though she hadn't had an easy life, she would always have fun. Like ice cream pleases the palate, good humor pleases the spirit, soul, and body.

It is important to make a special effort to laugh, such as watching funny programs. Laugh at life and you will conquer it! Keep the lemons out of your mouths. Speak good and look at the bright side. I think we should all have a "merry meter" installed.

There are times when we may be going through struggles or trials and may not be able to express what we are feeling in words. Or maybe there are times when we are feeling such love for the Lord that there are no words to tell Him. Maybe we are tired and stressed and feeling bad about not having the time to be in our prayer closet. Or, we are so "miscombobbled" that day that we just can't seem to pray ("miscombobbled" is my made-up word for *out of sorts*). One day when this happened, I spoke to the Lord about it. I felt He was telling me that He knows our heart, and that our heart is with Him. Every time we think of Him, He hears us. He hears our hearts just as much as our words. I think we've all been to that place where at times, we pray words, but they are just that — words that are rote and so routine that they've lost some meaning. And there are also times when our heart is so full that we don't need words. God hears our words, but He also hears our hearts, and I think that our hearts move Him even more than our words. God hears the cry of our heart. We also should not worry about always speaking perfectly. Moses couldn't speak well either. When a child prays, it's not eloquent. It's just from the heart. Words from the heart can be very simple. Eloquence doesn't matter, the heart does.

Sometimes we are so overloaded with things to do and burdens that we can't seem to get in the presence of the Lord. When this happened to me, I cried to the Lord and asked Him to let me know Him more. He showed me a vision of Him standing at a door, opening it for me and telling me to come in. It was a bedroom. He told me that I needed to rest. I needed to get back to that place of comfort and intimacy. I needed to get back to that place of dreams. It is a place of shared secrets, where lovers bare their hearts and souls. It is a place of *knowing* someone more than anyone else can know them. The way to know God more is to come into a place of rest with Him. We leave the cares and burdens outside the door. When we do this, we know Him and we get to know His heart. God does take care of our burdens, but it's not when we are overloaded with cares that we can find out more about Him. To learn more about Him, we need to rest in Him. That is when hearts are connected. When we are concentrating on worries, we are in our own little worlds. It is a time of *hardship*, not *heartship*. To learn more about God's heart, we lay our burdens down at the door. He already knows what we need, and then we trust Him to handle them. Then we come with Him and rest with Him. When we rest in Him, that's when we can hear His answers. John, the disciple, would rest his head on Jesus' chest. When we do this, we can feel and hear His heartbeat. That's intimacy more than friendship. Cares and busyness can take up our minds and focus so that we have lost our closeness with our Lord. He misses us when this happens.

We should never neglect our rest. It is what keeps us going. We can only go so long without it, physically and spiritually. When an engine is turned on all the time, it will eventually run out of gas. Stopping to rest will take us through and get us to our destination with energy left to spare.

My husband had a way of making me feel special and appreciated. He did the "big" things, but I especially liked the little everyday things he did, and he still did them after 40 years of marriage. He still opened the car door for me, and he would get the orange juice and make the toast for me when we ate breakfast at a buffet. He took care of me. It's not that I could not do these things myself. But I felt so special and loved when he did them. I appreciated the everyday things, but sometimes I forgot to tell him that I did. Do we remember to appreciate all the little things God does for us during the day? Do we remember to thank Him? Do we even notice them? Even though we may not realize it, He is always doing and working things out for us. I want to be more attuned to all the little things God does for me during the day. I want to notice them more and be more child-like; I want to notice that each thing, no matter how small, bedazzles me and I am in awe of

God. I never want to take what God does for granted. I never want to get "used" to it. It's true that we need to expect Him to be loving and kind, but we also need to be thankful and never take it for granted. I think that part of our love talk with the Lord is recognizing what He does for us and being thankful for the small things as well as the great things. I think it makes *Him* feel special!

Love talk: Don't *be* home without it!

Chapter 6

That F Word: Finances and Feuding

J was thinking about adding this section to the chapter on love talk, but when talking about finances, very often, there's no love involved. Feuding over finances is not fair when one speaks his or her mind and then won't hear the other's point of view. Married couples can solve any problem together, but together includes being three-corded with the Lord's wisdom and not leaving one of the other two cords out of the "together." Together means unity, not one always having its own way (1 Corinthians 13:4–7). It doesn't mean that if it's not done your way, you "take your toys and go home."

Our one granddaughter, who is three years old, sometimes doesn't like the way her big sister wants to play. The three-year-old, as three-year-olds do on occasion, wants her way. She's usually very easy going, but at times, in frustration, she will get mad, put her hands on her hips, and stomp away announcing, "I'm leaving!" She goes into her room and slams the door. She is cute at three years old, but isn't that what we do, shut the door to discussions when we want our own way and don't agree with our spouse?

Yes, we have the "right" to shut the door to the discussion when we've said our piece and we don't want to listen to the other's side, but isn't that controlling to get what we want? There can be no talk, let alone love talk, when there's a closed door between you. And even if, with other topics, there is no discussion, that one topic that's off limits shuts the door to complete intimacy and love that will sooner or later lead to resentment.

Money denotes power and the one that makes the money decisions has power and control. So many couples get married without ever having discussed finances. They are starry-eyed, never considering the consequences of two different financial viewpoints. Then after marriage, they find out they have two very different points of view when it comes to saving and spending. So many couples have such problems dealing with their finances that they get divorced as a result of this issue. Where did the love go? Money is so powerful that it can take over where love once was, if we are not careful.

Love is for better or worse, richer or poorer. Before we make these vows, we should not only have talked about these issues, but we should make sure that our love is strong enough to withstand the trials that every marriage goes through. Is the person or the finances most important? Can your love get you through the tough times?

Can you "love talk" even in financial decisions? Or is there arguing and struggling to get your point across? Or have you gotten to the point of being silent, yet you harbor resentment over the decisions made without your input?

Love is most important, but it takes *both* spouses to come to that realization for it to work in all the areas of life, including finances. Feuding over finances is never a winning battle. But if there is communication, not arguing, the conclusion that can be reached is that each one has their own strengths and weaknesses. When we see the value of each other's strengths, we can each have a role that will lead to victory. We can complement each other, even in finances.

Then we can change that F word from feuding in finances to fairness.

Chapter 7

Rituals: The Tie That Blinds

We all want to hear from God. But what happens when we read the same prayers over and over again, never changing the words? We get so familiar with them that we can repeat them without even looking at the words. It's not a bad thing to read a special prayer that helps us pray when we can't find the words on our own. Even Jesus taught us to pray The Lord's Prayer. What I am speaking about here is making "works" out of prayer, and not praying from the heart. We can read a prayer that really moves and touches our heart, and then because we were moved that one time, we will start to depend on that prayer and keep repeating it so much that it becomes ritual and rote, not even having any special meaning to us anymore.

It's the "garage" theory again. We hear God in the garage for the first time, and then we think that to hear Him again we need to be in that garage, that there is the only place He'll talk to us.

The way to hear from God is to speak from the heart. Saying rote prayers are rituals. We become dependent on the prayer and not on the Lord. We become as one who speaks and not communicates. I'm sure that the Lord, like us, would rather listen to a few words from the heart than hours of rote, meaningless speeches. Our prayers have become a crutch. They've become "works." When this happens, they also become bondage.

How many times has the enemy taken God's words and twisted them? He can also deceive us and make them into works. Works prayers don't work! It's exactly the opposite. Saying the same thing over and over again is not communicating. Prayers are talking to God, not giving Him a speech. When we start to put pressure on ourselves with *having* to say written prayers, then the prayers become more important than the Lord. Being in God's presence refreshes. Reading the same written prayers, thinking that reading them is what makes the blessing happen, is works, not faith. Faith without works is dead (James 2:17).

Works without faith is also dead. But "seek ye first the kingdom of God, and his righteousness; and all these things shall be added unto you" (Matthew 6:33). Communicate from the heart. A favorite prayer can be said from the heart. But repeating written prayers out of duty is not from the heart; it is dead works.

Many times the words can be the same, but it is the love and the heart that makes the difference with the result. For example, a husband can say "I love you" to his wife and look deep into her eyes in such a way that she can see the very love in his heart. Or, he can quickly say "I love you" without any emotion, and repeat it this way many times. Although he does love her and the words are the same, they are not as powerful. They don't have the same effect.

When we hear (and even say) the same thing over and over, how much do we really hear (and listen) after a while? Do we really listen as much? The Lord always hears our prayers, but I think His ears perk up when it's not the same old thing every day. Even the same needs can have fresh words. I know that God is not like us, but when someone tells me the same thing over and over again, it's ho-hum, here we go again.

To avoid any confusion, the Lord likes us to be persistent in our prayers, but that is not what I'm talking about. Persistence happens with the heart; persistence is not a performance or duty. It is not because we are so afraid that if we do not say these same prayers they will not get answered. It is not being afraid that if we don't say them, we will be attacked by the enemy. Fear is not faith and being afraid of missing a prayer is bondage. These are not faith prayers from the heart. They are duty prayers.

Fear can start to take control when we think that we can control the situation with ritual prayers. This is because we then shift from trusting God to do it to trusting what *we* do. We trust *our part* in saying the prayers to do it. This is putting faith in what we did more than in God. Our part becomes bigger. The speaking is the same. It's the reasoning or attitude adjustment that needs to be taken care of. Just because we speak the words does not mean that we are doing it. It is the power of the Holy Spirit behind the words.

Since we have authority in Jesus' name, I need to explain about authority so that we can have full understanding of speaking God's Word. In the father's house, a child can tell a servant to do something and it's done. But it's not done because of the child. It's done because of the power that the father has over that servant. It's done because of whom that child belongs to. The child has the authority to speak to that servant because of his father's name. The child has no power, the father does.

We can take the same prayer with the same words and not have the same power in those words. If we do not pray in faith, from the heart, knowing that it is not our "works" in saying the prayer that will bring the answer but that it is the power of God behind the words that does it, we will not see the result. This can very easily happen when we concentrate on what comes out of our lips, rather than focusing on the power of God's Word. This is so important to learn so that our efforts in prayer are not in vain and so that we will see the fruit of the words. We do not see the power behind the words if we are concentrating on the doing – the part that is coming out of our mouths – instead of concentrating on what God's words do.

We speak God's words with boldness and authority in His Name. He gives us permission to use His name, but it's still His power – the power of His Word – that does it. We have permission to use His Words, and therefore He puts His power behind them to work for us. The words may come out of our mouths, but the power is not in our mouths, but in His Word.

Learning this is important for two reasons. The first is so that pride will not enter in. The second is so that the words we speak will bear fruit. If we focus on our lips and our works, we will not see fruit. If we walk in the authority and boldness that God gives us, knowing that the power is not in what we're doing by saying them but in God's Word, they will bear much fruit. There is such a fine line of distinction here, but it is important to understand. Not because God is convicting us, but because unless we plug the cord into the right outlet, it has no power. You can hold the cord, turn the iron on and go through the motions of ironing, but unless the cord is plugged in, nothing we do will press the clothes, or bear fruit. When we can get this, our fruit will increase.

I say this from experience. One time, in particular, I let the enemy's deception cloud my thinking. I was working so hard, thinking I was fighting the enemy, when it was my own works tiring me out. God brought me back to my senses when He showed me a vision of the enemy just watching me punch the air and tire myself out. He did not have to wear me down; I was doing this all by myself. It's true that we have to do battle when the enemy attacks, but sometimes we don't realize he's taking it easy and we're the ones working when we don't have to. How is it that we can be so filled with knowledge and not have any wisdom?

When will we learn that doing without faith is actually putting up a wall of works or control? When we try to do things and take control with our works, we are like chickens with our heads cut off, scurrying about but accomplishing nothing. There's such a flurry of our activity, that there's no room for God to step in. When we step back and let God take control, we will see the answers. That way we will know that it is God that has done it, and not something we did. Sometimes we put more importance on doing than on the Lord.

When we use our prayers as rituals to make it happen, we will allow fear to come in. Ritual is works; faith is letting God do it with complete confidence that He does not need our help. It's not the prayer that is wrong, it's the reasoning behind it. When we pray in faith, we are praying for God to do it. It is very subtle when we start to pray as a ritual. We don't always realize it is happening. But when it happens, very slowly, we look to what we are doing by praying, and we leave God out. It's true that out of the mouth comes blessings and curses. It is true that we can speak over our lives. But there's a fine line. There needs to be balance. It's like a pendulum. When it is in the center, everything is balanced. But it can go to the extreme left or the extreme right. Extreme left is when we do not believe in blessings or curses, or that what comes out of our mouths can affect us. Extreme right is when we know that what comes out of our mouths affects us, but we try to do works by using our words to control things, thinking we are the ones doing it. It is taking God out of the equation.

It is good to declare God's Word over our lives. It is good to fight the enemy. It is good to speak blessings over ourselves and others. As long as we remember it is not us or our words that can do anything. It is the *power*, the Holy Spirit's power, *behind* the words that does it.

Works will burn us out and remove our joy. The Holy Spirit wants to give us new wine and bring back our joy. In the natural, wine dulls the senses and you forget your cares. It is false joy. The Holy Spirit's wine sharpens our senses and spirits and we see our cares become small as we look to the Lord. It's true joy.

All it takes is simple trust in God's Word. It's not about striving using His Word, just simple child-like faith. Speaking God's Word with that faith behind it will move more mountains than with works behind it. Works stems from fear. We can work and push that mountain all we want in fear, working harder and harder, and it won't budge. But a simple faith word will make it disappear (Matthew 17:20). Trust God. As God was teaching me this, I got the impression of raspberry tea. Child-like faith words will result in fruit answers.

It's not by might, nor by power, but by my Spirit, says the Lord (Zechariah 4:6). Running fast is fine, but there's a difference between running fast and running out of control. A tire on a car can go fast, but the driver controls where it goes. A tire loose, going down a hill goes fast, but it is out of control. With God in the driver's seat and the Holy Spirit in your "tank" (not a tiger), you'll win the race.

This chapter would not be in balance if I did not write about the times we have "extenuating circumstances." These are the times when due to illness, or extreme situations, we cannot be in our "normal" prayer closet. If we are rigid when these extenuating circumstances come about, we will break. Flexibility is the key. We need to bend so that our physical body does not break. At these times, we can trust God to know our heart for Him, and we can trust that He knows our heart in wanting to pray.

Coziness is the next step in the love relationship. We have to trust someone to let formality go and be cozy. By formality, I am talking about the need to be in your prayer closet exactly at the same time and place, regardless of circumstances, or you will not have peace. We have to let our sense of "protection" in routine drop for the familiarity of being together and being ourselves. That means if we are sick and can only say a short prayer, we can trust God to know that is the best we can do for the moment, and we can know that He still loves us, hears us, and answers. Love is when you trust someone to see you at your worst, such as when you are sick, or tired, or don't want to talk, and know that they still love you for who you are, when they see the "real" you.

For example, maybe every day you get up and make eggs for breakfast for your love, and one day you decide to stay in bed and hold each other. Which is better? They both have their time and place. They both are loving acts. We desire to talk to the Lord, but if for some reason beyond our control we can't be in our normal prayer closet, we can rest assured that He hears our heart. We can pray anywhere, anytime, whether short or long, and we can know that He hears us. A quick "I love you" during the day can mean as much as a long prayer of needs. Be free!

Chapter 8

The Holy Spirit's Love

The Holy Spirit is our teacher, friend, instructor, and comforter. He is the secret of our success! He lives in us; therefore, we have everything we need — in us. I think of the movie *The Wizard of Oz* and how Dorothy went in search of the wizard for answers. She found out that the wizard was all hype, all bells and whistles. What she needed was already in her. We have the Holy Spirit in us. He is everything we need. All our answers are already in us because He instructs us and gives us His wisdom. All we have to do is look to Him. Since He lives in us, we just yield to Him and He will give us the answers. He will lead us and guide us into all God has for us. It's already there; we just have to tap into it. Let go of the flesh part of us and let the Holy Spirit take over. When we do this, it's the secret of our success.

I happen to love using olive oil when preparing foods. God gave me an analogy about olives one day. He said that there are many people in this world, many "olives," but no oil. Some have never heard the gospel. Some have read the Word but have not understood. Then God showed me bread dipped in olive oil. He told me that His Word is bread and the oil is the Holy Spirit. Nothing is better than dipping bread in olive oil. Nothing is better than His Word being empowered (revealed) by the Holy Spirit. People can read the Word of God without understanding or revelation. But when the Holy Spirit is moving within them, they are given wisdom to understand it. Bread tastes sweeter with the oil. The Holy Spirit makes the Word taste sweeter and gives sustenance to their spirits as they understand it. It becomes real to them. It is food for their soul. He is our teacher and instructor.

I have found that when I pray, if the Holy Spirit is instructing me how to pray, my prayers are more effective. My words can be fine, but when the Holy Spirit gives me the words, they are more powerful and effective. I'd like to say that, without fail, every time I pray I have this instruction, but I'm not there yet. What I have found is that when I take the time to wait on the Lord, I actually "connect" with hearing Him faster than when I'm talking and talking and not making any progress in my petitions. All talk, no action! Even the "right" words, although good, are from the flesh, and "head" knowledge alone (without the heart) does not carry power. Words that have the Holy Spirit behind them carry the power to move mountains. They are much more effective than our "mountains" of words. It's not that our prayers are not heard. We should never be concerned about that. God hears the simplest heart — felt prayer. But I've found such a difference and know that my prayer has touched heaven when I'm guided by the Holy Spirit. Our prayers are supercharged when we wait and get direction and pray what the Holy Spirit tells us to pray. So wait, wait on the Lord (Psalm 52:9).

When we have the Holy Spirit in us, we will also have His fruit. Galatians 5:22–23 states, "But the fruit of the Spirit is love, joy, peace, longsuffering, gentleness, goodness, faith, Meekness, temperance: against such there is no law." There are times when I get so busy that I just don't have peace. Stress just seems to take over. It's then, when I reconnect and get in tune with the Holy Spirit, that peace will come. He is our refreshing, our living water.

The Holy Spirit also convicts us when we get off the right path. We should not think that He doesn't love us when He disciplines us and brings out things in us that need to be changed. It is *because* He loves us that He does this so that He can mold us and shape us to be the kind of person God wants us to be.

The Lord showed me a box of chocolates one day. Chocolate is easy to melt and mold into shape. If our hearts are soft, when the Holy Spirit points out an area in our lives that needs to be reshaped, we will melt easily. If we are hard-hearted, it will be more difficult for us to change. He wants to make us into fine chocolates, having soft hearts. All that is required is an open heart, a transparent heart, a soft heart — so that He can work in us.

We, as Christians, should always speak the truth in love. People may not always want to hear it because what they hear may make them see something in themselves that needs changing. The Holy Spirit has to deal with this as He speaks the truth to us in love. He speaks for everyone's good so that we can remove old garments of sin and put on clean ones. He has a hard job, but He does it for love. He is a friend that does not flatter or deceive, but a friend that we can count on to be truthful at all times, even when it is something we do not *want* to hear, but that we *need* to hear. A true friend is not a "yes" person, although that's what the flesh wants to hear. Like a true friend, the Holy Spirit will tell us when we are headed for a crash. He pulls us out of the mud. He doesn't wallow in it with us. What good would that do? He lifts us out.

The Holy Spirit polishes us so that we can have Jesus' light shine from us. He convicts us when we sin so that we know to ask for forgiveness, and He also will show us if we have a bad attitude in dealing with others. We all fall short; no one is perfect, and most people will not expect us to be. They understand failures. However, people need to see the Lord in us in the way we react to situations. They need to see His wisdom and instruction in us. They know we will make mistakes, but they want to see our attitudes, our "light," our humility in how we treat others. They will look for the Lord in us. That's why the Holy Spirit polishes us. He may show us things that make us feel uncomfortable, but it is to remove any dark spots. If people can see that we love them, they don't care how we've failed. So know that the Holy Spirit loves us and will do His best for us and in us, even if His polishing may "rub us the wrong way."

Having our rusty spots polished is never easy, but it's because of the Holy Spirit's love for us that He shows us the rust and polishes it out of us. We may not fully understand as we go through the polishing, but we will. Everyone that the Holy Spirit uses has to go through this from time to time. It's like the checkpoints for race cars. If they want to finish the race, they need to have a pit stop. However, the Holy Spirit always takes us out of the pit better than when we entered in. The pit stop exposes anything that needs to be changed and replaces it with what's needed to finish the race. Things are taken off that will slow us down. So stopping our moving forward (race), which we see as difficult and hard to go through, is only going to prepare us to go faster and finish the race in the end. Instruction and refueling comes when we are in the pit stop. Then we can move forward and with more confidence. If the Holy Spirit didn't love us, He would not change our tires. He would not give us new oil. Or fresh water. The old things have to go before the new ones are put in.

We will have many pit stops along the way, for on the road we can pick up many stones and we can burn out our tires. But the fire we go through in the pit stop is a refiner's fire, making us pure again. Refiner's fire is the Holy Spirit's polishing. When we humble ourselves, any pride or other "spots" can be burned off before they become a big problem. We get "cleaned up." I think of our granddaughter, Julie, not liking her first sponge bath. Sometimes we don't like bath time, but after we get cleaned up, we feel so much better!

The Holy Spirit is both powerful and gentle. He gave me an example to explain this contradiction in terms. It is like waves in the ocean: some are very powerful and strong, and some are very gentle and mild, but it is still the same ocean. There are times when we will see the Holy Spirit do big (dramatic) things in our lives, and there are times when He is like the gentler, smaller waves, guiding us in the little everyday things that go on. Sometimes the small waves are so gentle we can hardly feel them, but they are there. The Holy Spirit is always with us, guiding us, helping us, in the big dramatic things as well as the little.

I remembered being in Hawaii; the ocean was so warm and soothing. As the Holy Spirit bathes us in His presence, He is warm, soothing, and comforting. He baptizes us anew — a fresh infilling. It is refreshing, a fresh anointing. He wants to bathe us in His presence and fill us up. As a battery needs to be recharged, so does our spirit. We can't run a car on empty, and neither can our spirits. We need to recharge our spirits at times and be refilled and refueled. As we take time to just *be* with Him, He does just that. It's not selfish, it's necessary. In the natural, we usually will do for others first, then we take time for ourselves. It's hard for us to shift gears sometimes when we are so used to putting business, others' needs, and everyday tasks before being in His Presence. However, if we do not take time to refresh our spirits at times, we become dry with nothing left to pour out to others in need. Just as we need intimacy with our spouse in the natural, it is no differ-ent in the supernatural. We should not neglect taking the time to just love on the Lord. We get so busy with our cares and worries that we put Him on the back burner. We need a fresh breath of the Holy Spirit to revive us.

Consider the times we spend in instruction as makeover time. It's like at a health spa where the old skin is removed so that the new clear skin shows. It is where we are soaked. It is where we put good food inside (God's Word). It's where tight muscles are pounded and relaxing occurs. (The muscle part is the old flesh that bound up — bondages.) It's when old ways and routines are removed for healthier ones instead. It is to bring new life where it was stagnant. It's to keep us running (moving forward).

Sometimes old baggage is picked up so slowly that we don't realize it. These times can be hard, but if we are open and allow the Holy Spirit to work in us, we will be better for it in the long run.

One day in prayer, I was shown an old-fashioned soda fountain with an ice cream soda on the counter. The Lord was telling me to come to the fountain, that it refreshes. He was telling me to always put sweet things in me and to let the sour remain outside. That's why we sometimes need a makeover. A makeover in the natural is to bring youth to our bodies. A makeover in the spiritual is to bring back the freshness — the fountain of youth to our spirits. It is to bring fresh, clear, living water again to your spirit. Any impurities picked up along the way are removed. The "mask" is removed and all the impurities, the dirt, the blackheads and pimples, go with it. "Puffiness" around the eyes also leaves and we see pride go and humility will return.

Those that don't let the Holy Spirit do a makeover usually will get puffed up and fat and become unhealthy. They don't look good anymore to others and they don't feel good about themselves. However, after the makeover, they can look in the mirror again. There's a television commercial about mucous in the sinuses. The commercial is kind of funny, but that's similar to what builds up in us. It's the same principle. It's like the "little bad attitudes" move in. The Holy Spirit cleans house, but if His presence doesn't fill the room, they move back in again (Luke 11:24–26). These little demons of pride, bad attitudes, fear, discouragement, etc., are continually knocking on the back door with their old baggage. God's Word will keep them out. This can happen easily and subtly if our "me" becomes big.

Sometimes we go through these "makeovers," not because we are any different than before, but because God wants to give us revelation of ourselves in order for growth to occur. He exposes things in us that may have been alright before, but they need to be exposed to us now so that we can go to a higher level. At these times, it's not that we've actually changed for the worse; we're just seeing ourselves differently. The Holy Spirit has opened our eyes in order for change. That's why we may be feeling "miscombobbled" — out of sorts. The Holy Spirit is revealing things about ourselves to us, not for harm, but for good. He has greater things for us, but we have to change to handle them. For example, you cannot meet the king in rags. Esther was put in beautiful clothes and "cleaned up" for a year. She was being groomed to meet the king. We have salvation when we receive Jesus as our Savior and Lord. But we are constantly being perfected. It is a stripping of our old self, a peeling away of our old garments and of everything that is not of the Lord, so we can walk in all that He has for us. It's so that we can meet the King in our beautiful new garments. The Holy Spirit gives us revelation of who we are, and in Whom we need. He gives us revelation that we can do all things through Christ, and not ourselves (Philippians 4:13).

The Holy Spirit is also our comforter. If we come to Him in our sorrows, He can heal our wounds. He can soothe them with His ointment. When our hearts are broken, we realize something needs fixing and we come to Him. If instead we dwell on our wounds, they can fester and cause infection, even spreading throughout the body. Sometimes we may not even realize something is broken. It is only in humility and brokenness that we realize our need of repair. The Holy Spirit brings it to our attention and cleans out the wound.

God showed me a river with lots of trees and plants growing alongside, getting their nourishment from the clear water. They were thriving because of it. The river ran right down the center of this lush garden. Everything the river touched was bearing fruit; the trees were always in season. Everything the river touches prospers. If the Holy Spirit is in the center of people's lives, everything they do shall prosper. Psalm 1 states, "Blessed is the man that walketh not in the counsel of the ungodly. Nor standeth in the way of sinners, nor sitteth in the seat of the scornful. But his delight is in the law of the Lord; and in his law doth he meditate day and night. And he shall be like a tree planted by the rivers of water, that bringeth forth his fruit in his season; his leaf also shall not wither; and whatsoever he doeth shall prosper." If the Holy Spirit is the center of people's lives, everything they do shall prosper. He will lead them and guide them in every area of their lives. Their health, business, and finances will prosper with His direction. That is the secret. What is in the center of your life? Hunger and thirst in the natural are like hunger and thirst (malnourishment) in the spiritual. When the Holy Spirit is giving us our nourishment, God blesses us. He is our river of living water.

As you can tell by some of the examples God gives me, I love sweets. One cold winter day, I was in prayer, when all of a sudden, a warm cup of hot chocolate came to mind. I thought of how it warms us inside as it fills us and satisfies our body. It is comfort food. The Holy Spirit fills us and satisfies our souls. As we let the Holy Spirit's warmth in us spread to others, it comforts them. Our flesh can't do anything, but the Holy Spirit in us can. As we yield to the Holy Spirit, people will see God's love in us. "Not by might, nor by power, but by my spirit, saith the Lord of hosts" (Zechariah 4:6). As we show His love to others, how it must warm God's heart. And as we do this, we can be the hot chocolate for Him!

Chapter 9

The Thing in the Dungeon

During prayer one day I saw what looked like a dark dungeon door with a padlock. I got the impression that God was telling me that I still had hurts locked up inside of me. I needed to release my hurts, even when the person who hurt me did not say they were sorry. Otherwise the hurts will build up as they are pushed down deep inside and they are stored under lock and key. It's so important for people to say they are sorry. This is true regardless of whether we are the one that hurt someone, or the one who was hurt needing to hear those words. Otherwise these hurts build up so much that they take over our hearts. Then soon there is no room for love. And the door of that dungeon will also separate us from the Lord; He can't get in either. The result of that happening is that it is harder for us to hear Him. Once the padlock is broken, and the door is open, His love can flood in. Saying you're sorry right away, and meaning it, prevents darkness from building. It prevents separation from love. It prevents the enemy from getting ground.

So many times couples may say or do something that hurt one another because they are tired or overstressed. Many times, spouses don't even realize they did anything to hurt the other person. The enemy will use these times when we are weakened emotionally, physically, or spiritually because he can do his work easier. He can't accomplish as much when we are strong. When we keep in the hurts, it is the soil the enemy uses to grow his weeds of bitterness, resentment, unhappiness, and unrest. They are the thorns that choke out love. Love is most important. Saying we are sorry is a small price to pay to keep love alive and growing.

Sometimes these words are like undigested food that sticks in your teeth. But it doesn't take a boulder to remove it. Just a toothpick. A simple "I'm sorry" works wonders.

God showed me a walnut one day to help me to understand. He said the walnut is hard to crack. But once we do, the inside is soft and good. When someone is hard with us, it's just part of the outer shell that comes when they are tired and stressed. It is their protective covering. We should remain joyful and not let hurt or anger rise up in us when this happens. We need to remember that love is patient and kind. We should not notice when others do things wrong (1 Corinthians 13:4-7). It is all in how we perceive it. If we see the harsh words as darts of the enemy, we can make them fall powerless, or we can let them enter in and make us angry. Anger is contagious; joy is contagious. Both can take control. One is from the devil, the other from the Lord. How we react determines who gets control. This is a hard nut to crack, but once we do, it will be contagious.

These are not usually big hurts, but little darts that are used to annoy. They become like splinters or spines — prickles that not only cause pain, but that stick out of our heart so that others can't get close to us. The Lord wants to remove them. There are many types of "prickles." Fear is one. It is a prickle that torments. Fear has many splinters: fear of making mistakes or saying something wrong, fear of anger against us, fear of being hurt. It's like when you touch a cactus. There are many spines coming from one cactus. They are hard to see, but need to be removed because they annoy. And as we allow the Lord to remove them, people will be able to get closer to us.

When we are stressed, the stress blocks us from hearing the Lord.

It crowds Him out. When we are lost in a crowd of people at a noisy party, we have trouble hearing our spouse. This is similar to what happens when stress or fear comes in. We lose the Lord in the crowd of stress and fear. That's why when we are fearful and stressed it's hard to hear Him. He is still with us, but we can't find Him in the crowd. The fear and stress party has to be thrown out because they will not go willingly. And they are a noisy crowd! They drown out God's voice because they are so loud.

It's the same thing in marriages. Job stress, financial fears, even health worries tend to crowd out the pleasures of marriage, and some marriages fail. You can't hear each other over the crowd and you start losing each other in it. When you kick out the crowd and start embracing each other, you regain strength, have insight, hear the Lord, get answers and solutions — and hear each other. Stress wants to get in between you so that you can't embrace, so you can't hear each other. Stress wants to keep you apart. It's the same with the Lord. It's not easy to kick out stress, but when we do, we'll be amazed at the answers, at the sweet things whispered in our ears.

Congestion in traffic means nothing moves. Congestion of clutter — stress, burdens — means God can't move in us either.

Satan sneaks in gradually. He wants our prayers hindered, our blessings blocked. His modus operandi is this: Tired > Weakness in Spirit > Impatience > Blame > Hurts > Walls Between Each Other and God > Blessings Blocked and Prayers Hindered.

The Lord loves us even when we "goof." Shouldn't we also love our spouse when they goof? I should think that one way we show our love to them is loving them when they come home tired, impatient, and stressed, understanding that it is not directed at us, giving them the freedom not to have to be perfect at all times.

God usually teaches me by analogies or comparisons. One day, He showed me a flower. He said the center of the flower is like the heart. Everything important takes place there, and production of seeds for reproduction is one important thing. If a petal is removed, it will not destroy the flower, but if the center is damaged, it will die. When the enemy wants to destroy us, he attacks the heart with hurts. He knows that is our vulnerable area, for it supplies the very root of our being — our spirit, hope, and self-worth. His tools are other people that he works through by anger, misunderstandings, and miscommunications that can stem from past bad experiences. He's so crafty that people never know that it is him doing it. He works as an undercover agent, for if we could see him doing it, his tactics wouldn't work. Red flags should come up when anger arises. When people are "tuned in" to the Lord, they will actually know that deep inside, they don't want this anger in this situation, but sometimes they still let it control them. Little by little, if they take control over the anger, they will see victory.

Most of us have had plenty of practice being hurt. And each time we get hurt, we learn more about how to handle these hurts. However, sometimes if it's someone that is a new friend to us, we tend to start back at square one, and when hurt, we are tempted to fall into a new resentment. The people who hurt us may change, but the way we handle it should not. We need to be aware of two things: the enemy's strategies and our flesh. Let our spirits rise, and not our flesh!

What happens when we have forgiven people and even loved them when they hurt us — when we have given the hurts to the Lord, yet the hurt is still in the "dungeon"? Our love is not always enough to remove them, only the love of God is. Though we release them to Him, we've released them mentally, not spiritually. It was a mental choice, however now we have to release them from our heart. That's when the Lord can heal. It may take us time to do this. In this case we need not only our love for the person, but we need to receive the Lord's love for them. It is a supernatural love. We need this supernatural love especially at times when the person who hurt us does not apologize or admit it, or when they keep repeating the same hurt to us. These are hurts that are locked in the dungeon and only the Lord's key can remove them. These hurts are the most difficult to go — the unjustified, repeated, unapologized for hurts. God does it in His timing using His type of heart surgery. First we choose to release them to Him mentally, and then we allow Him to open our "dungeon" so we are able to release them to Him from our heart. It takes His supernatural love to do this. He can even use the hurts for good, teaching us and helping us to grow, giving us wisdom.

True love is when you love a person not for who they are as much as for who He is. Let His love reign in us. Our flesh can't give us the love we need for people when they hurt us, only the Spirit of the Lord can do that. Is Jesus in your heart? Then you will have love for others. Then you will see the best in others. You will see then through Jesus' eyes. You will stop looking at their faults, as Jesus stopped looking at yours. You will see the good in them, as Jesus saw the good in you. This can't be done in our own flesh or by our own power, but by the Holy Spirit and the love of Jesus in us. Walk in His Spirit and not in the flesh. If we succeed in rising above the hurt, we have blessings. When we think well of and look for the good in others, even when they have hurt us, we are protected from sickness, poverty, or whatever else Satan would try to put on us. We have taken away his legal ground. Hanging onto hurts, grudges, or bitterness — thinking the worst of others — hurts us more than it hurts them. It's like when we have a vase of flowers. It needs the old water to be changed because otherwise it gets smelly and stagnant. Sometimes what is inside of us has to be drained so new can be poured in. We need to be emptied of the old — and sometimes we can feel as if we've been drained emotionally and physically — so that we can make room for all that God wants us to be. Otherwise we are too self-contained and our "me" is too big. So take it to God, and get over it!

We need to remain joyful, even when people are against us. For when we let their critical thinking and negative words get the best of us, we behave badly and give the enemy legal ground. That is exactly what he wants. We have to put up a shield and let it roll off our backs, because rolling with it will only do us harm. What is more important? Holding grudges or receiving blessings? We should not let anyone stop us from moving into what God has for us.

God was teaching me about this one day as He showed me what looked like a spot where a wart had been removed and was now gone. Warts are like barnacles on a ship that slow us down. They are the past negative things that attach themselves to us. But the Lord scrapes them off like barnacles of a ship. When they are removed, we can move fast into all He has for us. Warts are the surface negative things that attach themselves and stick. They are superficial annoyances, prejudices, and injustices done to us, to name a few. How we react will determine if they stick. They stick if we react with anger and let it fester. We need to take these things from whence they come and not let them "get to us." If we forgive right away, it won't stick. Then there will always be smooth sailing and no barnacles to slow us down. There will always be negative, critical people in this world. We should not receive their garbage. We should not let it form warts or barnacles to slow us down or steal our joy. People may try to negatively affect, hurt, or wound us. Misery loves company. God wants to remove these hurts and negative garbage that have been thrown at us so that we can move forward.

Hurts are especially hard when dealing with family. Satan will use family because we are emotionally tied and it is hard to break through. He uses the "big guns" when he uses family to come against us. We should not fall for it. We need to keep our eyes on the Lord and our lips from speaking evil. Blessings and strife do not go together. Which do you prefer? This is so important. If something is done against you, leave it in God's hands. If we let it roll off our backs and have joy in the midst of it, if we trust the Lord to take care of it, we will be pleasing Him. We should not be smart in our own minds, for if we do not try to work it out in our own way, He will work it out in His.

As previously stated, most times when people hurt us it's because of how they are feeling, what someone else did to them, how they were treated by someone previously in a similar situation, or it is because they are overtired and under stress. Most of the time it has nothing to do with us. As we grow in understanding of this, we will learn not to let others control how we feel, for that's exactly what happens when we become hurt. They have controlled how we feel, and if we dwell on the hurt, it gets bigger. Choose to turn the other cheek and have joy. Overlooking it will benefit us more than dwelling on it.

We can be on the "lookout" for hurts or injustices, and we'll always be able to find them. Or, we can be on the "lookout" for the good in people, and we will find joy. There are always those who, if there are two ways to take something, will take it in the way that seems to insult them. We don't choose for people to hurt us. But we can choose the way we react to it. HURTS… **H**ow **U** **R**eact **T**o **S**omething. Just put the blood of Jesus over the hurt and let it *Passover* you! Give the hurt to the Lord. He can deal with it better than you.

Jesus says that we abide in Him, and He in us (John 15:4). So when we hurt, He hurts, too. His love heals all wounds; we just have to let go of them and give them to Him. He can't take care of them if we don't give them to Him and let Him fix them. So often we ask Him to heal our hurts, but then we don't let go of them. Suppose a child had a wheel fall off his toy truck. He asks his daddy to fix it and the daddy says that he will. But the child won't let go of the truck or give it to his daddy to fix. Daddy can't fix it until he holds it in his hands. People pray so hard and so long, but they don't surrender the hurt to the Lord.

One day the Lord asked me why I get hurt so easily? Is it because of a soft heart? Is it because I never want to hurt anyone else, so I really feel bad when someone hurts me? The Lord is hurt many times by people He loves. How does He get over it? He has great love for everyone. No human can fathom it. He brings each one to greater levels of love, each according to one's own experiences. He then reminded me that I asked Him to give me more love for others. I remembered, but I thought He was just going to put more love in my heart for them. (Of course, that would have been the easy way for me.) What He said to me next was that loving someone when they are perfect is easy. It doesn't require great love. Loving someone when they hurt you requires greater love. Selfless love is getting our minds off ourselves and our hurts and not turning inward when hurt. I then wondered if doing that requires a toughness or hardness of heart. But the answer I got was that it just requires the hurt to be let go. He then gave me a picture of a soft heart and an arrow piercing through it. Hard hearts can't be pierced and hurts bounce off. But they also can't have great love. Soft hearts will be pierced, but if we let the arrow-hurt pass right through, it goes quickly. If we don't let it pass through, it stays inward and keeps our mind on the hurt.

I then asked if it were better to have a heart that is pierced easily, or a hard one that isn't pierced at all? Love requires an open heart, a soft heart. The greater the love for others, the quicker the arrow-hurt passes through. We should not dwell on hurts, for it only causes harm. Why are we hurt so easily? Because to become Christ-like, we need to open up our hearts, and when they are open, love as well as hurts will come in. Let love stay, let hurts go.

I thought of the word fortitude. We need fortitude to learn how to withstand the attacks and not let them get us down. It is different than hardness of heart. In hardness of heart, nothing can penetrate it — nothing is allowed in. Fortitude is having the strength to remain soft-hearted and not let the attack do damage.

Jesus taught us to bless those that curse us (Matthew 5:44). It also states in Romans 12:14, "Bless them which persecute you: bless, and curse not." For when we speak blessings on our enemies, we really are speaking blessings over ourselves. What we give out will come back to us, pressed down, shaken together, and running over. We think of that scripture in terms of money, but I think it can relate to anything.

So often, as children we are very sensitive and can't bear to see suffering of any kind. So we put up a protective shell. Then during the early years, the shell becomes thicker as our hearts are hurt. We become like the clam, opening up the shell when we think it is safe. We protect our heart at all times, always on guard. Sometimes the shell is hardly open at all. And if each time we try to open it a crack we get hurt again, we will keep it closed for longer and longer periods of time. Jesus wants us to put our hearts in His hands; He wants us to trust that He can heal the wounds. He can heal so that the shell is not only able to be opened but removed. He will not just help us in dealing with any new hurts but give us complete healing. He does this by allowing Him to get through the shell — to get to the old hurts — and remove them. He wants to bring emotional restoration to us. We have to know who we are in Him, to receive all He has for us. Therefore, restoration of what was lost *of* us will lead to restoration of what was lost *from* us. Emotional restoration = physical restoration.

The body is composed of water and salt. When we taste someone's tears, we are brought into their very being. Jesus collects our tears in a bottle. When we have intimacy with Him, we taste His tears also. There is intimacy and transparency. It is a trusting of emotions. Jesus sees our tears. He holds us in the night cries and has been there for us in the day. He is there when we shed tears of joy as well as tears of sorrow. He's held us in His arms even when we didn't realize He was there. He tells us that weeping may go on for the night but joy comes in the morning (Psalm 30:5). However, we have to let go of the hurts to make room for the joys. If a heart is already full of hurts, it can't hold joy; there is no room. We cannot do this on our own, for it is not by might, nor by power, but by my Spirit, says the Lord (Zechariah 4:6). When the hurt is taken away, then the space can be filled with joy. The Lord wants to use us as His vessel, but "baggage" has to go. We can't be consumed with our needs, problems, and hurt and also be used to help others. We have to clean out the garbage so that love can fit in.

Just as hurts have to be let go, so do past negative experiences that have led to wrong thinking and mindsets. These have to be taken out of the dungeon and released. Before we can move into the promises of the future, we have to let go of the past. It's almost like the movie *Groundhog Day*. It is as if we can't seem to break out of the past repeating itself.

I have read that if a baby or child does not get the love of his parents by a certain age, it is difficult to be replaced. We perceive things by relating them to past experiences. An example of this is when a mother tells her son that big boys do not cry and continually embarrasses him for doing it. He will grow up shoving his emotions inside, fearing ridicule and rejection if anyone sees him crying. Yet, Jesus cried for His people. However, people usually don't look to Him as their example. Their perceptions generally come from past experiences with their parents when behaviors were being formed. If all a parent did was ridicule and criticize, when the boy is a man, he perceives things as criticism that others would not. How do we learn to let go of past experiences that would keep us living in *Groundhog Day*?

When we realize that we have the Spirit of God in us, we realize that we have Jehovah- Jireh, Jehovah-Rapha, Jehovah-Shalom, El Shaddai — all that God is — in us. Therefore, no lack, no sickness, no worry can enter in unless we let it. The past should not be allowed to control our thinking or our future. Where the Spirit of the Lord is, there is liberty (2 Corinthians 3:17). When we realize this, we can, with great faith, tell lack, sickness, or worry to go. We can be so confident that no evil shall befall us nor any plague come nigh our dwelling (Psalm 91:10).

We can either become bitter or better. It's a choice that everyone has to make at some point in their lives. Bitter feeds the flesh with junk and the body waxes thin. Better feeds the spirit with goodness so that the body gets strong. The Bible is the instruction book. We can read it, but we have to choose to take action and follow it. Jesus is our role model as well as our Savior. He showed us what to do, and then died because He knew we would fail as we learned. So the key and secret for us is to learn to love even when others fail or hurt us. Isn't that what Jesus did? If we can do this — and we need Jesus' help — then our "dungeons" will be empty of hurts and negative thinking and we will be full of love.

Chapter 10

To "C," Or Not to "C": That is the Question

Control — it's that seven letter word that is more like a four letter one! It gets us into trouble all the time. What we should control, we don't, and what we shouldn't control, we usually try to.

Several years ago, God showed me a balloon. He told me that He was using the balloon to teach me about control. He wanted me to do better at not trying to control situations, but to give Him control to handle them. He told me that if I held onto the balloon, I would have it, it's true. But if I "loosened my grip" and let it go, it could go higher than I could see. God wants to take us higher and bring us into all the good things He has in store for us. He has more for us than our eyes can see. If we remove the weights of control off from us, we can go higher.

How many marriages are suffering because there is a spouse that controls? For example, suppose a husband sees his wife as a possession instead of a partner, and therefore he controls. When a man sees his wife as a partner, he values her opinion, and there is intimacy. However, possessions can't give intimacy, partners can. A woman knows her husband loves her by the way he treats her. Does he treat her as a valued treasure, a gift from God? He can say he loves her, but the proof is in the performance. A woman who feels loved and valued will put her husband's desires above her own. A woman who is treated as a possession and is controlled will feel she has to fight for her own desires and needs. This is just as true for the wife that tries to control her husband. Love is the answer. Just follow the instructions: love is patient and kind and does not demand its own way (1 Corinthians 13:4–7). If Jesus rules in us, we have love and we can love our spouses as He loves us.

What about when we have a different opinion than someone else? Giving an opinion different from someone else's is not trying to control that person. However, expecting someone to have the same opinion as you or else you get offended, is. That is not a relationship, it is a dictatorship! Everyone should be allowed to have their own opinions.

Transitioning from child to adult can also be a source of growing pains for both child and parent. Sometimes grown children have a problem seeing themselves as grown and independent from their parents — or even worse, they think the parent does. (Which may be true in some cases.) When this happens, it can cause a problem when the parent gives an opinion. Grown children may feel like they have to take their parents' advice. They think that the parents are controlling them, when the parents are just treating them as they would if they were talking to a friend about a situation. When this type of thinking occurs, it can wreak havoc in a family, with the parents being afraid to say anything that could even be construed as an opinion. In this kind of situation, the grown children can be the controlling ones and not even realize it.

What about the parent who does try to control grown children? Generally, it seems it's the mother who has more trouble letting go than the father. There's even a term called *empty nest syndrome*; although it does not necessarily include control, it can have that affect. This is especially true if the mother and father have centered their whole lives on the children to the point of never taking the time to do things for themselves, just the two of them. Then they have nothing to say to one another when the children leave the nest. They may have forgotten how to "love talk." This can be very scary for the wife if she feels that her whole purpose in life has just left. I think it may have the opposite effect on the husband, who has had to be "second fiddle" since the children came along!

Last summer, I watched as a mother bird was making her children leave the nest. She would shoo them out, at which time there was a lot of loud "protest" peeping — a very noisy commotion that went on for days. One would think that the mother bird was being mean, but if she didn't do this, her babes could not learn to take care of themselves. They would always be dependent on her.

Love is freedom; control is bondage. To love someone is to give them the freedom to grow. To control is to put them in bondage. They are bound to what the controller will allow them to think, or feel, or do. There is no growth with bondage. Even authority shouldn't try to control. Authority is to guide and lead for the purpose of growth. My husband and I are so blessed to have a pastor who is happy to see his flock growing and going to higher levels, even if it means them traveling or moving away because of their calling. That is non-controlling authority. It's the same as parents not holding their children back from pursuing their dreams. Parents who love their children enough to let them pursue their dreams have their children's best interests at heart.

The Lord loves us. He does not try to control us. He gives us a choice in everything we do. I've learned that when I choose to give Him control over my life, He works things out much better than I could. I've learned over the years that worry does me absolutely no good. I used to be the top "worrywart" and could worry as good as the best. In fact, my husband used to say that I was not happy unless I was worried about something! That is, until I learned about God's great love for me. It did not happen overnight, but as I started to leave my cares in His hands, I would see how He worked things out. The time spent worrying was wasted and could have been put to better use.

One day as I was worrying over something (it was so insignificant I don't even remember what it was), God said that He just wanted to tell me that He loved me. He said He wanted to tell me not to worry, for He is in control. He then showed me His hands. He told me that they were big enough to handle everything, and that I needed to trust Him. I then remembered how Bill used to take my hands in his to pray over me and how I felt so loved, so safe, under his protective covering and love. I realized that is how God loves and cares for me. At that point I felt so silly to have worried and thanked God for His love and patience with me. When we realize His love for us, we know that we are in His care, and that we never have to worry about anything. Just put it in His hands and give Him control over it.

So the moral of the story is that with human beings, control very often is that four letter word. But with God in control, the four letters spell *love*.

Chapter 11

Please Pass the Salt

The Lord loves us all, with our different opinions, thoughts, and feelings. In fact, He made us to be different. So why do we sometimes compare ourselves to others? Or think that God must love Johnny more than us? We look at others and think they must be more "spiritual" than we are, however, we don't see the whole person. We just look at their "perfect" parts and think: Why can't we be like they are? We see them at their best.

We should never wonder if we could lose His love. He knew us before we were born and He loved us then. He knew what we would say and do (Psalm 139). He even loves us when we put our foot in our mouth! Jesus told Peter that he would deny Him three times. Jesus knew he would do this before Peter could ever imagine that he would. Yet Jesus still loved him.

The question then comes to mind: Are we Christ-like enough in our love for others when they "deny" us? When they don't understand our feelings, thoughts, or actions? When they are not exactly like us in our ways or our thinking? Peter learned from Jesus. Maybe we, too, can learn from others as Jesus teaches us and opens our hearts to see that not everyone thinks or acts or feels the way we do. Understanding is not one-sided, but it would certainly be a lot easier on us if everyone thought the way we did!

We are each different, each of us having our own flavor. What good is salt without its flavor (Mark 9:50)? There are different kinds of salt, and different kinds of people. Different people see beauty in different things. Some like country, some city. What's beautiful to one is not to another. I can be upset with people who don't think as I do, or I can understand that no one is going to be exactly like me. Not even our spouses think the same as we do all the time. In fact, it is good that they do not. Men and women think differently and communicate differently. God will show our spouse something that we don't see and show us something that our spouse doesn't see, but it is all for the same purpose or goal. He gives each of us a different part of the puzzle, but it all fits together perfectly. We can't complement one another if we always think exactly the same. One's weakness is made stronger by the other, and vice versa. We should not despise our differences — the different ways we think or communicate. Those differences make the whole. In an egg, the white and the yolk are different, but what would the one be without the other.

We choose not to be angry with other people's opinions. If we are angry with everyone who doesn't feel as we do, we would not keep our friends very long. No one is exactly like us, and we shouldn't expect them to be. One secret of happiness is to not let hurts bother us. We should understand that everyone is made differently and has different life experiences and different ways of thinking. If we just do our best for them, that is all God asks.

People will always be going about their businesses. What matters today may not matter tomorrow. Cares will come and go, and people will come and go. But the one constant is God's love for us. Is it really important what one person's opinion is of us? And what good will come from criticizing another? Thinking may change from day to day. So we should not put our efforts into what others think or do, or their opinion of what we think or do. Just look to the Lord and care about what pleases Him. For God does not change, nor do His thoughts toward us or His love for us. People will do what they do, or say what they say, or think what they think. These things disappear like smoke. We should not let these things affect us. Be confident in the Lord and who we are in Him. That's what pleases Him. That's what keeps us moving forward.

Aren't we being perfected to be more like Jesus? Jesus loves us with our different opinions, thoughts, and feelings. For example, if we were all doctors, there would be no one to teach, and so on. Yet we are to be the same in love. God's Word says that love never notices when others do things wrong. It is forgiving without holding grudges. Love understands even if it doesn't agree with the other's point of view. Love *allows* the other to *have* a point of view different from their way of thinking. And we may even be surprised as Jesus helps us learn from one another. If we only see things our way and expect others to see it that way, too, we are self-limiting and controlling. Jesus wants us free.

It all starts with revelation of His love for us. As we see His love for us, we will understand and have more love for others. When Jesus' love fills us up — when our "tank" is full — then that love will spill over to our relationships with others. People may look different on the outside, but all have hopes and dreams for their lives, and for their children and loved ones. When we understand this, we will relate to our spouses in a more loving way and we will be open to see things from the other's heart. We will not be so quick to judge or criticize, or to jump to wrong conclusions. When we are secure in Jesus' love for us, we will value ourselves. We will be open-minded enough to see people of other cultures and countries worshipping the Lord with songs and dances different from what we know, and not criticize or think our way is the only way. The Lord likes variety! Why else would He make each one of us so different? It's a freedom in which people can love Him and express their love for Him in their own way.

I asked the Lord for an example of this to better understand. He showed me a house with one main electrical box and many wires connected to it — one for the oven, one for lamps, one for the dishwasher, etc. They are all connected to the main electric box, yet all are for something different. The box can handle it all, but the wire cannot. But they both have the same purpose: to bring electricity to it. They are both connected. People may each worship the Lord differently, or one may have a heart to help the poor, another may have a heart to take care of the sick, and someone else may have a heart for souls. Not everyone can do everything. But they all are connected to the Lord, who can. Each person's heart is connected to the Lord's in a special way, each with desires matching God's heart in a different area. Each one is a little different, but all are connected to the Lord.

We need to be set free from religious spirits that make us think that our way is the only way — or the best way — and that is better than anyone else's way. Jesus' heart is moved by people's genuine love for Him, not the particular song they sing. Yes, it's true that we all have our favorite songs, the ones that move our hearts. But we shouldn't look down on others for what moves *their* hearts. David's wife, Michal, was disgusted with him as he danced and sang before the Lord, but God was pleased (2 Samuel 6:16). How we must miss out when we put our "blinders" on! I wonder what it will be like in heaven with people worshipping the Lord, each in their own way, and children dancing and singing unto Him, expressing their love for Him in the simple ways only children can. What joy! What freedom! I can almost see the Lord smiling as I think about it. Why do we keep ourselves chained to our old ways of thinking or doing things here on Earth? Why do we remain closed-minded when there are so many things to learn and understand? Jesus says, be free!

What about when we feel different from others, or maybe even insignificant? Jesus showed me a blade of grass one day. A blade of grass seems insignificant, but each blade is important to the lawn. We may not notice one blade missing, but when several are missing or diseased, it leaves a bare spot on the lawn. Each soul is important to the Lord. He doesn't want any to be missing or diseased. So many people feel insignificant. They think of themselves as useless because they are not a great scientist or a top CEO. They may not be as successful in a way the world deems successful. Yes, there are those that rise to exceptional greatness, but all are significant in God's eyes. The helpless child, hungry or dirty, has God's love as much as the CEO. The diseased and bedridden are just as important to the Lord. His desire is for everyone to be a part of a green lawn: those that have, helping those that have not. The sick well, the hungry fed. No matter who we are, or what position we hold, He loves us. He desires for us to be the best we can be, whatever that is. We hold a special place in His heart. Help the little children and those in need, and pray for the sick with boldness and authority. So many feel insignificant and even sorry for themselves. But the way to be significant is to help someone else. If you are poor, you can still pray, and encourage and spread God's Word. If you are rich, you can supply food, shelter, and clothing. The only way to be insignificant is to not do anything when you are able to do something. Yet even those who are not able to give, or to pray, because they are too sick, are significant, for in their weakness, God is made strong. They also cause others to be strong as they help them. No one — no, not one person — is insignificant to the Lord.

We may have a different flavor than someone else, and we may act, think, or be different than others, but He loves us all. So to be different may be to add flavor. Please pass the salt!

Chapter 12

'Til Death Do Us Start: The Love of Jesus:

I wonder if we can ever understand the magnitude of the love that Jesus has for us. We are the bride of Jesus. Just as we feel whole and complete when we marry our spouse on Earth, so it is with Jesus. We are made whole and complete as we are in His presence and are one with Him.

The heart represents love; breath is life. When Jesus died on the cross, He gave up His breath for us. His natural heart stopped beating for us. He did it because He loves us. Every heartbeat, every breath speaks our name. He bought us and we are part of Him. We are His.

When I picture Jesus' heart, I see light bursting forth from all around it. His love is the light of the world. Those that have the love of Jesus have His light shine from them. Those that walk in darkness do not know what the light is, but they are drawn to it. They know that there is a difference about people with this light. They know it as goodness, but they don't know the source. They see the surface, but not the power and love behind it. It is the Holy Spirit that will give them revelation and let them see.

We let the love of Jesus rule in our heart, for what the heart contains will show on the outside. Love lets our light shine. The more love, the more light. As we open our hearts to the love of Jesus, He pours in His love and it shines so brightly it affects our outward appearance.

We will have joyful lips, sparkling eyes, radiance. It doesn't come from makeup or skin care; it comes from the heart.

Jesus' light and love are with us at all times. We may not "feel" it at all times, but it's there. We are just flesh, and have emotions of the flesh, and sometimes we let these emotions take over our spirits. But Jesus' love is with us no matter where our emotions take us. Jesus showed me an example of this. First, He was with me on a porch swing. Then He was with me on a seesaw. He told me that no matter where we are, He is with us. He is with us whether we are up or down. He is on the same "board" with us. But like a seesaw, when we are down, He cheers us up. He also told me that there are times when He is sad, too. No one really thinks about Jesus getting sad, but He has feelings, too. However, whether we know it or not, when He is down, we can lift Him up. We do this by being with Him and loving Him. We can even make Him laugh. He needs our love just as we need His. The relationship is not one-sided. Are we sensitive to His needs?

Jesus wants to meet our every need. One day as I was praying, I saw a bell on a ribbon by a doorway. Jesus usually shows me pictures when He wants to teach me something, so I asked what this meant. Many years ago, when the master of the house needed something, he would ring the bell and the servant would come. Jesus said that as we ring the bell of our hearts and seek Him, He comes. He meets every need, every desire, and every cry of our hearts. I was confused about this because I am *His* servant and I want to meet His needs. Then I felt the Lord asking me if it gives me pleasure when I serve my children or husband? Or, when I serve those I love? He said then I would understand how it gives Him pleasure to give to those He loves — and yes, even serve them. Didn't He wash the disciples' feet (John 13:4–15)? His desire is that we love Him. Do we love Him? His desire is that we obey Him. Do we obey Him? His desire is that we are kind to others. Are we kind to others? His desire is that we give to those in need. Do we give to those in need? Then we serve Him well! It's mutual admiration.

We all want to do our best to please the Lord, but we are imperfect and we live in an imperfect world. Sometimes we are so afraid of failing or making the Lord mad that we allow the devil to put fear and condemnation in us. But by being so afraid of failing, it means we don't trust His love for us. We believe the devil's lies more than Jesus' love for us. We equate the love of Jesus with the human love and experiences that we have had when people failed us by getting angry or not forgiving us, or even leaving us. We think that if we make Him angry, we will lose His love, the closeness that we have with Him. But that's nonsense! People may fail us, and they may not forgive us when we fail, but they never died or shed their blood so that we could be forgiven, like Jesus did for us. He has *invested* in us, and when you invest in something, you do not throw it away. He will never leave us. He will never stop loving us. The flesh may win a battle, but Jesus has won the war. We should not let Satan put fear in us that Jesus would separate from us. It cannot be. He will not separate Himself from us. Only we can make that choice. It's like a lock on a bedroom door. It only locks on one side. The person on the other side can't lock it. Jesus will never lock us out. His door is always open. His arms are open wide.

Jesus once asked me why I was still afraid and allowed fear to come in, even after I asked for forgiveness. I answered that I was afraid of losing the closeness I have with Him, or that He would be mad at me. His response to that was to ask, "Do you trust Me?" Of course I said yes, but still He said, if that were true, why didn't I trust Him to forgive me right away? Why didn't I trust Him to understand me? Why didn't I trust that He has unconditional love for me? He told me that I saw Him as human with human love. He said that I equate Him with a person, one who may not forgive right away, or even at all. He asked, "Don't you realize that I don't just *say* that I forgive you, like people do. I *acted* upon it, and suffered and died for it." Forgiveness has been done already. He's taken care of it. Past, present, and future sins have all been forgiven — all just for the asking.

I also wondered about when we fail over the same issue again and again. He reminded me about Paul in Romans 7:15–25, when Paul said he couldn't do what was right no matter how hard *he* tried. The flesh will fail over and over, but as Paul wrote in verses 24 and 25, "O wretched man that I am! who shall deliver me from the body of this death? I thank God through Jesus Christ our Lord. So then with the mind I myself serve the law of God; but with the flesh the law of sin." Jesus died in His natural flesh for the sins of our flesh.

We have "new-humanship." Jesus died for us once, but we receive the result of forgiveness again and again. We are continually being made new in Him. It's like a time capsule, because forgiveness is always there at the time when we need it. It's the gift that keeps on giving!

One day after a failure, I was feeling very broken, like Humpty Dumpty when he fell off the wall. I was broken and not able to put the pieces back together. I had egg on my face! It was then that I realized that, many times, God can only work with the broken. He can't always work with those on the wall, those who have it all together on their own.

Sometimes when we fail, we think everything has gone up in smoke. God showed me a cigar that I saw as smoking, but He showed me that the cigar was really made of bubblegum. He told me that His plans cannot go up in smoke. Sometimes things happen and we have to "chew" on them for a while. Bubblegum can either stop you up when you swallow it, or you can chew on it and blow bubbles. However, if, in the natural, we are proud and are not humbled as a result of the situation, we get puffed up and blow our own bubbles. We are full of wind. When we swallow our pride and humble ourselves, rather than being "stopped up" as we would in the natural, God takes away what we swallow and fills us with His Wind — the Holy Spirit. And as His

Wind blows bubbles, they will not pop and cause our face to become sticky. They will not cause us to lose face and be ashamed.

The Lord cleans us up as we repent. Then as we step back and trust Him, He shows us what He will do for us. Not because of our goodness, but because He wants to show us His goodness and His love for us. We've all seen His goodness when we do things right. But, at times, Jesus will show us His goodness, even when we have messed up. He does this not to reward us, but to show us that He loves us even in those times. It's one thing to know He loves us when we are good, but He wants us to know the deeper love He has for us. How many of us can remember times when we did not deserve the Lord's goodness, and yet He came through and rescued us anyway! After those times of failure, we may have felt so empty, but that emptiness resulted because we had gotten rid of ourselves. Then He fills us with His love. As we see what He has done, we are then filled with a greater love for Him. We get a fresh revelation of His love for us. And as He puts His love in us, we will have more love for others.

One of the hardest things we have to do is learn to forgive ourselves. I think that it may even offend Jesus when we feel guilty after we've asked Him for forgiveness. And then we even feel guilty about feeling guilty! What a vicious cycle we take ourselves into. We are disappointed in ourselves for failing. Disappointment is an emotion and it is alright to feel sorry that we failed. But when we ask for forgiveness, it's done. On the cross, Jesus said, "It is finished." The hardest thing to learn is to let go of our emotions about it and accept that fact. Once we ask for forgiveness, it is taken care of. Most of us already know this, but it is in *doing* what we've learned that gives condemnation the boot. We need to move on, otherwise we waste time fretting. It's just like a baby in the womb: the parts are growing, but they are not complete until birth. We knew we had the parts, but after birth we learn what to do with them. When we are learning in the spirit, we know about failing and Jesus' forgiveness, but when we "birth" in this area, we learn how to handle failures and not let guilt control us any longer. Freedom from disappointment, guilt, and condemnation are birthed in us as we come to maturity in our trust in His forgiveness. It pleases Jesus when we don't keep chastising ourselves, for it shows we fully understand what He did on the cross. In the natural, we think we have to keep "paying" for our sins by feeling bad, otherwise it wouldn't seem that we were sorry enough for it. But Jesus would say to us that *He* already paid for it, so ask, receive, and move on. In the natural, each year is celebrated as a birthday. In the spirit, I think that each victory, each revelation that we act on, is a birthday. Birth is the time when we learn to act upon what we've learned. It is the completion of it in our hearts.

One day, the Lord showed me a birthday cake with one candle on it. I was wondering why there was only one candle, as at my age, the cake should have been ablaze! In the spiritual, it is different from natural birthdays, when the years add up and we get older. In the spiritual, when we are reborn, there is one candle forever, for our spirits do not age like the flesh. The one candle represents the one soul that is born of the spirit. So at our rebirthday party, there will always be one candle. Each year, as well as every day, is a new beginning. His mercies are new every morning. And on Earth, every day is a new beginning — a fresh start — putting past failures behind and growing in the spirit. In eternity, there is no beginning and no end. There is joy and gladness forever.

I used to make Christmas ornaments that were made from a plastic ball or heart shape that came in two halves. When I made these ornaments, I not only snapped the two halves together, but I glued them and put a ribbon around the seal. They could not be taken apart. The two pieces could not be separated. It's like that when we give our hearts to Jesus. We cannot be separated. We are sealed together. Forever. One. Jesus wants us to know His love for us is just like that. On Earth, we wear His engagement ring. I once got a vision of Jesus putting a gold wedding band on my finger. Then I felt He was saying, "'Til death do us *start.*" When our flesh dies, we start our eternal life as Jesus' bride. We are His bride forever.

The truth is that if we are barefoot (always transparent and exposed) with Jesus, He will keep us pregnant with His promises. We will "birth" all that He has for us!

As I wrote earlier in this chapter, sometimes it's hard for us to imagine Jesus' great love because people will disappoint us and fail us. People very often will not expect Jesus to have a great love for them, or that He knows their hearts or their wants and needs. They relate to Him as a result of experiences with other people. But sometimes the opposite is true also. People will very often expect other people to know exactly what is on their hearts because they relate human knowledge to the Lord's. For example, how many times is one spouse disappointed because the other didn't know what they wanted? They expected them to "read" their mind. It is so easy to fall into that trap. The answer is to ask the Lord to help us get it right — to not expect too much from others, but to expect the Lord to do great things!

To summarize, we also can expect to fall short now and then. But we can expect that it won't separate us from Jesus' love. We just need to understand our shortcomings and learn from them. Perfection will only come when we are in heaven with Him.

We may be disappointed in ourselves at times, but Jesus is not disappointed in us because He sees the end result. He knows the end and how it will turn out. He doesn't look or judge or react as a man who looks at what is going on at that moment. He looks at what we will do in the end. Psalms 139 says that the Lord knows what we are going to say and do before we do it. He scheduled each day of our lives, so He knows the outcome and how it will work out. He understands that we feel bad when we fail. But we don't need to chastise ourselves or believe the devil's lies. We need to just come to Him and say we're sorry, and it is done. Sometimes the flesh can condemn as much as the devil!

Expect from Me
Not humanity
For all you have
I give to thee
Do not put your faith in woman or man
For though they do what they can
They will fall short in many ways
In what they give and do and say
But I will always come through for you
So trust in Me, you won't be blue
I Am the reason for the season
The only gift that is a pleasin'
I Am the One who satisfies
The Bread of Life who never dies

Jesus is our Shepherd and we are His sheep. He tends us and feeds us with His Word, and cares for us. He guides our paths. And He also shears us so that the heat will not bother us. When the enemy attacks (heat), the shearing (trials) prepares us to withstand.

When we go through trials, Jesus is right there with us. It's like when we are in a tunnel of love with our mate. When we go into the darkness, our mate draws us closer. When we go through the darkness, Jesus is sitting right next to us. It is in times of darkness that He is closest to us, and He draws us closer to Him. There will always be light at the end of the tunnel, for He always turns what the enemy meant for harm, to good. He holds us in His arms in darkness as lovers do, and when the darkness ends, we are closer to Him and stronger than when we entered. So we should not despise the darkness, for we will come out from it better than before (Romans 5:3–5).

My child, do not fear
For I, the Lord, your God am here
I work in ways you cannot see
It's My Spirit that surrounds thee
I keep you safe from all harm
My Spirit is a soothing balm
So in the spirit you must see
That I give you victory

One of the most intimate things we can do with someone is to dance with them, the kind of dancing that is slow and romantic. As we dance, we are touching, moving as one — connected. Quite a while ago, as I was praising the Lord, Papa showed me how He danced with me as a child — letting me put my feet on His as He supported me. Then a few years later, I saw myself dancing with Jesus, with my feet moving alongside His. He was showing me that I was growing, so that my feet were alongside His. He was leading and directing my paths, but my part was now hearing His directions and going where He leads.

I remember a television show that my family used to watch when I was a small child. It was *The Jimmy Durante Show*, and at the end of every program he would say, "Goodnight Mrs. Calabash, wherever you are." I have heard, although I can't be sure, that she was his wife that had died. His love for her was so great that it must not have ended when she died. The Lord loves us wherever we go, wherever we are. His love is always with us. The Lord's love for us will never die. There is no place that we can go to get away from the love of God. His Word says, "Whither shall I go from thy spirit? or whither shall I flee from thy presence? If I ascend up into heaven, thou art there: if I make my bed in hell, behold, thou art there. If I take the wings of the morning, and dwell in the uttermost parts of the sea; Even there shall thy right hand lead me, and thy right hand shall hold me" (Psalm 139:7–10). He loves us here on Earth, and that love will be known to us in a greater way in heaven as His bride.

'Til death do us start!
Come into My secret place
A place where you can see My face
A room that is all aglow
And I will tell you things to know
It is a room that's filled with light
And warmth that radiates — it is bright
The joy in there has been untold
Unspeakable love will unfold
So come with Me into this place
I welcome you into My space
Walls of diamonds, sparkling gems
Reflect beams of rainbows out from them
Floors of agate, chairs of gold
Wealth and riches I behold
Yet humbly in the midst of all
I see My Savior standing tall
He reaches out His hand to me
And on His wrist, nail scars I see
He left these treasures to become
The sacrificial Lamb for one
And in that room now I can see
The brightest One of all is He.

Chapter 13

Don't Be a Turkey! Thankfulness

*I*n the United States, we set aside one day of year for Thanksgiving. We celebrate with turkey and all the trimmings as we think about all of the things we can be thankful for. But some have started to drop the thanksgiving part of the day and call it "Turkey Day." The feast becomes more important than the reason behind it. We certainly can't feast like that every day, otherwise we would become obese. But we can be thankful every day and not get fat. In fact, when we are thankful, it prevents us from becoming "puffed up."

The Pilgrims were Christians — God-loving and thankful to Him. People have so much more today, yet instead of thankfulness increasing in proportion to the blessings, it has often decreased. There are more blessings, but less thankfulness. Human nature tends to never be satisfied. It is only God's Spirit that satisfies. It changes thinking because of love. When we are filled with love, we are appreciative of what we have and want to give to others. When we are filled with love, we do not want for ourselves, but we want for another. So the focus should not be on the turkey — not "Turkey Day" — but Thanksgiving Day. And Thanksgiving Day should be every day.

Thankfulness shows the Lord that we love and appreciate Him, and that we think of Him and do not take Him for granted. It shows that we acknowledge Him and have not forgotten Him. People sometimes think that as they wait for God, He's forgotten them. He has not. But how many forget Him? Or forget to thank Him when He blesses them or answers them?

Expectation has two sides. On the one side, expecting and trusting God is good when it is also combined with appreciation and thankfulness. Expecting God's blessings and goodness pleases Him because it shows that we trust Him. It has nothing to do with greed. That's where the enemy tries to deceive us into not asking for our needs to be met. As long as there is appreciation and thankfulness to God for what He's done, it is not bratty or selfish. And as long as we share with others when God blesses us, it's not greedy. Thankfulness pleases God — not because He needs to be thanked for Himself, but because it shows humility and that we do not have pride or give ourselves credit for what God has done.

On the other side, expecting because we think that we deserve it is not good, for then it is combined with greed and selfishness. This type is never satisfied. It always sees and wants more.

Thankfulness is becoming rare. If children expect they will get everything they see (I'm not talking about needs), without the appreciation of the hard work it took for their parents to give it to them, then how can they learn to be thankful to God? I sensed in my spirit one day that God was weeping for these children who know no sacrifice, for how can they understand His sacrifice for them? No, God has not forgotten them, but I think He may wait so that they can learn how to handle what He gives them without getting into trouble. God wants to teach them responsibility. If children are just being given, without being taught responsibility, they get into trouble. Keeping up with the "Joneses" and what they give their children materially may mean keeping up with your children getting into as much trouble as the Joneses' children! It doesn't always come out as physical trouble, but can be emotional or spiritual trouble as well.

Immaturity can stem from childhood selfishness that never was allowed to mature due to spoiling. This can lead to selfish attitudes and unappreciativeness. The word *spoiling* can be taken literally, because sometimes it can cause them to go bad. A demanding child that parents cater to will spoil. It's like giving sweets to them until they get sick. They want, but if they get it all, it will cause sickness. Parents have to know when to stop giving just because the child wants. Giving does not replace love. Love wants to give, but love is also discipline to do what is best to help the child grow. Love doesn't give out of guilt. Gifts do not replace love. A child that only receives never learns the joy of a giving heart. It becomes, instead, a selfish heart that equates love to a gift, yet thinks they are the only one to receive.

The difference is *how* we receive. Receiving with appreciation will not cause spoilage. Receiving and expecting that we deserve it, with no regard to the cost of what it took to give the gift, causes spoilage. The amount of toys never satisfies. The amount of love, does. I have seen children who have nothing receive a small toy and respond by showing they are so grateful. They never expected it and are so awed by having it. Children with toys lavished upon them start to expect them, and if denied, they rebel. Where is the balance? Too little breaks the hearts of parents. Too much destroys the spirits of children who are never satisfied. What would happen if each child gave a toy to one without any?

Please and thank you are the words
That open many doors
Use them often and you'll see
Increase upon your floors
Your barns will fill, your silos too
You'll see them overflow
Just use these words and you will see
Prosperity where you go.

Thankfulness can only come about by love. Giving shows love, but it can't be one-sided or else it can cause spoilage. Appreciation and thankfulness have to be on the receiver's side so that giving can come full circle. The person receiving, seeing love, wants to give out of that love. It is being thankful. Can we do this in our flesh? No! It's only by opening our hearts to the love of Jesus and receiving His gift of love to us that we want to share gifts of love with others. Our flesh may rot (spoil) in the grave, but not our spirits, because of Jesus' love for us. Do we receive it? Do we appreciate it? Or are we spoiled?

Giving to our children is good — we all want to give because we love — as long as they realize the sacrifice it took to give it, whether it be the extra work, or denying getting something for ourselves. Isn't that what God did for us? He gave His Son so we could live. Jesus suffered so that we could have forgiveness, health, prosperity, etc. Do we just expect, and not appreciate, the sacrifice of what it took to give to us?

Sacrifice is only a sacrifice if it is done out of love. Then the sacrifice is a joy. A sacrifice that is done grudgingly is not a true sacrifice, because the reason behind it is not out of love. We may do it because we want to look good in the sight of others, or for martyrdom, because we want pity, attention, or sympathy. It is about "look what I've done," and not about the helping someone else. It's the "poor me" attitude behind what is being done. When you sacrifice or do something for another, the "I love *thee*" has to be greater than the "I love *me*". If you do it for what you will get out of it, then it's more for you than it is for them.

It's the heart, the intention, the motivation that moves God's heart, not just the act. We could spend the money we give on ourselves, our desires, and our needs. It's not the amount that matters so much, but the fact that we give when we don't have to, and we give when our own desires may not have been met. It's the sacrifice. There's more joy in blessing others out of love than out of "duty." Blessing others out of duty may be the right thing to do and it pleases God, but blessing others out of love — just for no reason — gives Him joy. We feel more joy, too. That's the secret!

Sometimes we don't see or recognize the little things that God does for us. We may look to Him for the big needs or think that it is God only when we see great miracles. All the little things go unnoticed. I remember how my grandmother would always make things special. She did not have much, but she would take a piece of material or some small item and make a pretty decoration for a package or a homemade doll. The Lord loves to make things special for us, too. Do we take the time to notice the small things?

A small gift in season, just like a word in season, does wonders. I am blessed to have a good friend that always seems to come through with what is needed, and at the right time and the right season.

This person has the gift of knowing exactly how to bless someone at their time of need. I've seen my friend do this time and time again, whether it's through a word of encouragement, a card, a meal, or a timely prayer. Many times, it will be a book, tape, or music CD that will be so perfect in helping that someone who is going through a hard time. It's the little "cup of water" that can lift a spirit. Touching just one soul — having a heart for even one — touches God's heart as well. Sometimes the little things are easily overlooked, yet very often, the little things mean the most. And then, when we give to another, they, in turn, will give thanks to God for the blessing that they received (2 Corinthians 9:12).

Humility has to come before love for others can enter. A prideful heart only has self-love. Love for others comes from humility. God will not usually move us up unless we step down first (Luke 14:8–11).

If our heart is closed to the small, it becomes closed to it all! In the beginning when we first come to the Lord, we are thankful for every small blessing. We notice everything. Sometimes we need to go back to our beginning, to remember the small things and be thankful for all things. And like my friend, we should not forget to do the small things for others. And who can say that a little insignificant thing we do for someone won't impact their lives greatly. If we keep our heart for the small, we will always recognize the blessings we receive, and our hearts will not be hardened. It's always the small things — the things we don't see or notice — that trip us up!

Thanksgiving is a time when people in the United States give thanks for all of their blessings and for all of the blessings upon this nation. The Lord loves it when we have thankful hearts, but it must sadden Him that it is very often just for a season. Why can't people's hearts feel this way all year? Are hearts dictated by the calendar? Is giving just for Christmas season?

I felt God's heart one day as He spoke to me about this very thing. It's true that these times are made special, but Jesus came to Earth to show people His love all year — always. Celebration of His birth at Christmastime is a good thing. I think God likes birthday parties! But love and kindness to others should not stop when the party's over. Those that have true joy in living — and giving because of love — will have more and more joy, and more and more thanksgiving. Giving begets joy, joy begets thankfulness, thankfulness begets giving and more joy. A merry heart does much good (Proverbs 17:22). Therefore, the joy of the Lord is our strength. Strength is all encompassing — steadfastness, strong in mind, strong in body, strong in faith.

What pleases God is the way we handle what He gives us. God does not *lease*, He *gives*. When someone gives, it belongs to the person that it was given to. However, the person that it was given to should not take credit for getting it. That's where the danger lies. That is wrong thinking — to give ourselves credit (or glory) for it. As long as we know that every good and perfect gift comes from the Lord, then we won't take credit. Even the job we do to earn money to buy what we want comes from God. But God *gives* us these talents and abilities; they are ours. Everything we are and have comes from Him, but it is a gift, not a lease! We will have it as we give the glory to God for giving it to us. It's called thankfulness, and thankfulness is not proud. A person with pride isn't thankful because he gives himself credit.

My sacrifice is what I give
In order that you may live
And as you sacrifice to Me
Many blessings, you will see
It's selfless love to sacrifice
Instead of getting something nice
To give to Me instead of self
Is the secret of great wealth
I will always bless you more
Than what you could ever store
So as I sacrificed for you
Be kind and bless some others, too.

Chapter 14

All in the Name of Love

Jesus shed His blood so that we could live. You see, life is in the blood. Sin is death — there can be no life eternal with sin. That is why before Jesus came to Earth: God's people needed to sacrifice the blood of animals, to offer the animal's blood for their sins. When Jesus came to earth as flesh and blood, He died — shed His blood once and for all — to cover each person's sins so that they would have life eternal. The blood of animals could not do this, only God's own blood. Since God is Spirit, He had to come to earth in human form. He created flesh and blood, and now He had to become it to save what He created! When there is no blood in a person, he dies physically. There can be no earthly life. Without Jesus' blood, there is no life eternal. Life is in the blood. Why did He do this for us? He did it in the name of love.

One Christmas, I was asking Jesus what He would like, and I felt in my spirit that He would like a birthday cake. The world tends to put aside Jesus' birthday and just make Christmas a holiday to exchange presents. However, Jesus was born knowing that He would face an excruciating death. He did that for us. As we celebrate His birth, we realize that He came for our rebirth in order to spend eternity with Him. He gave the gift of His life so that we could have eternal life. Can any gift compare to that? Giving is good, as long as we remember the greatest gift — Jesus' love for us. Jesus loves giving gifts and watching people receive them. But giving should be because of love, not duty or to outdo anyone else. Giving should just be a simple gift that says love. A simple treasure from the heart means more than a truckload of duty or tradition. When we give out of a heart of love, we give to Him also, for He is Love. His birth was a true gift of love. If we receive nothing else, receive His love.

Christmas comes but once a year
It comes and brings us great cheer
Not for the presents under the tree
But for the One who came for thee
It's not for jewelry, gloves, or tie
But for the Babe who came to die
So we'd have life eternally
The gift He gave to you and me

My child, this Christmas day
Remember what I had to pay
I came to Earth, was born of flesh
To give you life — from My death
Although it happened long ago
There is one thing that you should know
For you, I came from heaven above
I did it in the name of love.

During prayer one day, Jesus showed me a field of candy canes, and I remembered Christmas as a child: the smells of the tree, baking, and the familiar decorations. But mostly, I remembered running down the aisle at church, feeling Jesus' great love for me. I didn't have to look for Him or strive — He was just there. I could feel His presence. A candy cane is like a shepherd's staff: It has a hook on one end. A shepherd uses the hook to draw the sheep to him when they start to wander. At

Christmas, people who don't know Jesus' love will feel love for others and be drawn to Him because of that love. They may not even realize what or why they are feeling this way, but Jesus put the love there. There are so many candy canes, yet right after Christmas, they dissolve and disappear. Jesus' love never leaves. Why do they?

I love the scenes on Christmas cards — usually so peaceful. Yet, so often, Christmas is not peaceful at all. People are stressing out and trying to make everyone happy. However, making people happy is not our job. When people look to the Lord, He gives them joy. That's the part of Christmas that people take out of His hands. They make it their responsibility to create happiness and the "perfect" Christmas — the perfect gift, the perfect meal, the perfect decorations. We should take our eyes off those things, for Jesus is the perfect gift. It's about Him. We can't create joy with all the things we do, for Jesus gives true joy. So don't let these other things consume us. Let Jesus consume us, and then we will have joy. It's nice to make our house look good, and to give a gift to those we love, but people have taken it to extremes and it then becomes stressful, not fun. Relax, and see if He won't fill your stocking with joy! More stuff, more stress, more mess. More Jesus, more happiness!

Jesus' birthday's not the time for stressing
Or, My child, to be depressing
It is a time to feel great joy
To celebrate the Baby Boy
Who came to give eternal life
And joy and peace instead of strife
So my child, be of good cheer
Your Savior, Lord, and King is here!

The Christmas before my husband went to be with the Lord, he gave me a beautiful bracelet, but it was what he wrote beneath it that meant most of all. He wrote: "For a Lifetime of Love." As I was thanking God for blessing me with Bill, He told me that silver and gold are precious, but more precious is the love in the heart. That is the true meaning of Christmas.

Christmas is the season of giving
It should represent the life you are living
And giving out of a lifetime of love
Is what I did when I came from above
This is the secret of true Christmas spirit
Giving not out of duty, but love that is in it
Silver and gold is not the true treasure
But a lifetime of love is great beyond measure
You've just received the best gift of all
A husband who treasures your love most of all
Not watches or cars or big television sets
But a love that has grown since the first time you met
And words that are written deep in your heart
Do not fade or corrode or be torn apart
For love is the one thing that will last forever
It is the greatest gift — eternity's treasure.

Our life here on Earth is temporary. It is our training ground, or boot camp, so to speak. Our fleshly body is only like that of an astronaut's space suit. It protects us from the elements of Earth, while we are on this training ground. But life on Earth is temporary to prepare us for eternity. Jesus wants as many people in His boot camp as will come.

Some people think that life on Earth is their end-all. They think of it as their beginning and their end — all there is. Those that have never been told about Jesus don't realize this life isn't the end. Some may have head knowledge that there is an eternity, but they don't really know what to believe. Some were never told, and some don't want to believe or receive. They have been hoodwinked by the enemy's deceptions. They are in his "prison camp" needing to be freed. Jesus has freed them. The prison doors are unlocked, but they don't know that they can get out. They are blinded. It's like a pet that's been kept in a cage all its life and one day the cage door is left opened, but the pet doesn't know he can get out. He needs someone to call him and say, "Come." Who will call them? The door is opened. Who will say "come"? Jesus' love sets them free.

Jesus has poured out His blood upon us. He has invested His life for us. How then could He ever give up on us? He knew us before we were born; He's chosen us, and then He died for us. There is no turning back. He will never change His mind about loving us or choosing us. He's already done it. He didn't suffer and die because we were going to be perfect. He did it because He loved us even when He knew we could not be perfect. So if He did all this for us even when He knew we would fail, why would He ever change His mind and stop loving us? There is no time with the Lord. He knew us before we were born (past), He knows us now (present), and He knows our end (future). It's hard for us to imagine, for we only know the present. We can't conceive it — all we have to do is believe it!

The Lord wants us to know that we may have been through many trials, but as we are faithful to Him and do not give up, we become like pearls, treasured by Him. We are beautiful to Him. He can take the roughest grain of sand and turn it into a thing of beauty. There is no one — no, not one — who has done anything too rough or ugly that He cannot change. He wants us to know that nothing is too filthy for Him to touch. Didn't He touch the leper? No past is too dirty that He won't clean it. Satan may whisper in our ear that we've gone too far down into the gutter — but he is a liar.

Maybe you never knew the Lord. Maybe you're wondering if He wants you. The answer is YES. Suppose you were shipwrecked: Would you try to just save the children who knew you? Or would you try to rescue all? The Lord wants to save you. He wants to put you in *His* eternal lifeboat. He loves you. All you have to do is *choose* to receive His love. You don't have to live in fear or bondage. He has already won the victory to set you free.

The Holy Spirit is whispering in your ear right now. He says that all you have to do is call upon the name of the Lord. Just say Jesus, and He will hear. He will wash you with His blood and make you clean. He will transform you and do for you what no one else can do. He will take you from pauper to prince, from Cinderella to princess. He will take your filthy rags and put on a new clean garment. You've tried in your own strength. Now take His. He reaches out to you and says, "Come."

I love you more than life itself
Not idle words, put on the shelf
Nor just words that I have said
My flesh has torn — My blood has shed
Some do not know why I went through
The suffering that I did for you
And why I came down from above
I did it all in the name of love.

To receive this new beginning, pray this simple prayer:

Lord Jesus, I believe you are the Son of God. I believe you came to earth and died on the cross for my sins. I ask you now to forgive me of all my sins. Come into my life, be My Lord and Savior, and I will follow You all the days of my life. Thank You for giving me eternal life, and thank You that now I am born again. Amen.

Postscript

I had finished writing most of this book when the love of my life, my husband Bill of almost forty-one years, went to be with the Lord. It was a very quick illness (cancer) lasting only about two months. It seems fitting to me to speak of him in this postscript, as he was the epitome of what love is about. God truly blessed me when He brought the two of us together.

We met on a blind date. I told my parents not to even bother to meet him, as I would probably never see him again. But God had other plans. Bill said that from the first date, he knew that I was the one for him. We were very young when we got married — 18 and 19. Bill and I worked hard. We attended college and then Bill went on to law school. (Bill was working and going to school at the same time and graduated with honors.)

Bill was a man of integrity and honesty. The most important thing to him was to do the right thing in God's sight — to always be able to "look himself in the mirror." From the moment I met him, he was able to solve problems and care for others. He was the most generous man I have ever met.

Before we were married, he told me that, together, we can do anything — and we did.

Our love was very special. I knew that few people had a love like ours. We were each other's best friend, lover, cheerleader, and encourager. His colleagues have told me many times over the years that they never heard him speak a negative word about me — nor did I of him.

He was my life and I was his. I could always count on him whenever I needed him. He was always there for me. Even after almost forty-one years, he would send me love notes and flowers, and always thought to bring me one of my favorite treats when he came home from work.

We loved spending time together. We never tired of each other. When we first met, we had a year away from each other in different colleges, and it was torture. We always considered it a luxury to be near one another. We were so much a part of each other. Before Bill went to be with the Lord, he said I knew him better than he knew himself.

He still opened car doors for me and loved giving me special gifts. He really waited on me and spoiled me, and I loved it. For our twentieth wedding anniversary, he surprised me with a trip to Hawaii and had arranged for us to renew our vows. He adored his children and grandchildren and felt so blessed. I can remember when our daughter was very young, toy Smurfs were very popular. One day he was at the mall and saw a huge stuffed Smurf that was almost her size. He bought it, put it in the front seat of the car, and drove home. Many other drivers chuckled as they noticed it. Our daughter was so excited to receive it.

He was a man of great faith. I cannot remember a time when it was shaken. Even through this illness, it remained strong.

He encouraged me in whatever I did, and never stopped me from attaining my goals. He believed in me.

He had a heart for his clients — always doing his very best, always being truthful with everyone. He was a perfectionist and would not give up until they got his best.

I was always amazed at how he knew so much about so many things. He had a genius IQ — and a humble spirit. He never thought more of himself than he did of others. He was a giver.

There were many words given that Bill would be healed. Bill and I knew he would be, too. God gave us the same word about five different times from as many different people, including myself, that he would be healed. So I did not understand at first when he went home to be with the Lord. But then I began to understand. It was a short illness, but a very painful one. A few nights before Bill went to heaven, He was awake at night praising God and Jesus came walking into the room. Bill felt such joy and peace as he heard His audible voice, telling him that all is well, he is healed, he is saved, and He was waiting for him to do good things. Bill said several times after that night that he would never forget how he felt at that time and what Jesus said. The next few days he was in excruciating pain. When I reminded him of Jesus' words, he told me that he could never forget the joy and peace he had. He said that if it was that good for only the few minutes he spent with Jesus, he wanted to be in heaven to experience that joy and peace all the time. He said his work was in heaven. After he went home, I kept asking God why Bill wasn't healed, and I finally got a revelation. In the first book God gave me to write, *Lessons I Learned From The Lord*, there is a chapter on death. In it, God spoke to me and said that He speaks life always. But that life can be life on earth, or it can be life in heaven. Either way, it's life. And healing in heaven is the ultimate healing. I had forgotten this, and I could almost hear Bill say — as he did so many times when I struggled: "Ev, read the book!"

His life is a testimony of God's love. I was so blessed to have a man like him. He was a rare and precious jewel. He always told me he would love me forever and longer, so I know I will be reunited with that love in heaven. A love like ours never dies.

I went to his office a few days after he went to be with the Lord and under the glass on his desk, I found something I had written to him a few years ago. He saved all my cards and letters to him. It just seems right to say this again:

For all the times you've been there for me —
I thank you now

For all the times I've laid my burdens on you —
I thank you now
For all the things you've done for my family —
I thank you now
For being my strength when I didn't have any —
I thank you now
For being my encouragement when I didn't have any —
I thank you now
For believing in me when I couldn't —
I thank you now
For knowing all my faults and loving me anyway —
I thank you now
For being the best husband, friend, and lover in the
world—I thank you now
For all that you are, all that you do, for being you —
I will always love you.

Other Resources

Books
Lessons I learned from the Lord
Walking in the Spirit-There's Power in the Wind

Blogs
Read and/or sign up to receive Evelyn Lang's encouraging, insightful blogs at evelynlangbooks.com

Made in the USA
Middletown, DE
19 August 2020